W9-CIQ-875

Parliament and Public Spending

The Expenditure Committee of the
House of Commons, 1970–76

Ann Robinson

Lecturer in Politics,
University College, Cardiff

HEINEMANN · LONDON

Heinemann Educational Books
LONDON EDINBURGH MELBOURNE AUCKLAND TORONTO
HONG KONG SINGAPORE KUALA LUMPUR NEW DEHLI
NAIROBI JOHANNESBURG LUSAKA IBADAN
KINGSTON

ISBN 0 435 837508

Published by Heinemann Educational Books Ltd
48 Charles Street, London W1X 8AH
Filmset in Great Britain by
Northumberland Press Ltd, Gateshead, Tyne and Wear
and printed by
Richard Clay (The Chaucer Press) Ltd,
Bungay, Suffolk

Contents

105255

Acknowledgements

I would like to thank the Social Science Research Council for their financial support for the research on which this book is based; Miss Juliet Merrifield who collected much of the background material and conducted a number of interviews with Members of Parliament and Civil Servants; and Mrs Vilma Flegman who assisted with the collection and analysis of material from reports of the Expenditure Committee. The research would never have begun without the support of the University of Bath and the encouragement of Professor Cedric Sandford. I would also like to thank all those Members of the House of Commons, Clerks of the House, Civil Servants and Specialist Advisers to the Expenditure Committee who generously gave their time to provide interviews. Few of them will recognise their own individual ideas about the work of the Expenditure Committee which have been woven into the text of this book. The author, however, owes them a debt for stimulating the thoughts expressed here.

Ann Robinson
Shirenewton, Gwent
October 1977

Introduction

This book considers the relationship between control over the financial affairs of Government and the locus of political power. It starts out by making the assumption that those who are able to make, or to influence, decisions about public spending have thereby an important asset as a basis for power in politics. Not all significant political decisions are concerned with money, of course, and some that are relate to taxation which is not dealt with here. Nevertheless the assumption that to take part in or to influence the making of public spending decisions is to have a share in political power seems to be more and more valid as the scope and volume of Government spending grows. If we can discover where control of spending rests, then we will begin to understand something, if not everything, about the locus of power in the political system.

More particularly, this book considers the relationship between two specific elements in the British political system: the Government and the House of Commons. Its central concern is to evaluate the ability of elected representatives to take part in or to influence, and thus to obtain power in respect of, the public spending decisions of Government. One aspect of this book which is perhaps novel in studies of the respective roles of Government and Parliament is the great stress that is laid on the need to examine their relative roles within the context of all the other pressures working in the determination of public spending decisions. For this reason, although no attempt is made to provide equal analysis of all of the many elements in the public spending equation, attention is drawn in Chapter One to the need to consider Government and Parliament not merely as two sides of a power equation, but as two bodies exercising relative amounts of power over the course and patterns of public spending within the constraints imposed upon them by the many pressures from economy and society. The examination of the actual work of the House of Commons which forms the bulk of the book is concluded by referring back to the framework set in Chapter One to provide 'a new view of Parliament's power of the purse'.

The main substance of the book is an empirical study of what Members of Parliament actually do when they are engaged in the practice of controlling public spending. Since 1970 the main forum for Members of Parliament to take part in detailed scrutiny and control of Government spending proposals has been the Expenditure Committee of the House of Commons, and a case study of its work from its establishment in 1970 to the end of the 1975–76 session of Parliament forms the bulk of the book. By presenting evidence of MPs' behaviour when confronted with the opportunity to debate or to investigate Government spending plans and proposals and by estimating the degree to which they make full use of their opportunities, it is possible to provide some indication of the extent to which the House of Commons contributes to the process of deciding who gets what of public spending. On the extent to which the Expenditure Committee realises its potential rests the ability of the House of Commons to hold 'the power of the purse' over Governments and to influence the course of public spending.

There are two main sources of information used in the case study. Firstly there is analysis of documentary material. On the general control of spending by the House of Commons as a whole the main source of evidence comes from the material contained in the Hansard reports of the debates in the House. The main source of documentary evidence about detailed control of expenditure comes from the reports and minutes of evidence published by the Expenditure Committee (see Appendix B). These now run into many thousands of pages and many millions of words. They are a valuable source of evidence not only on the behaviour of Members of the House of Commons but also on the links and communications between government departments, pressure groups, and Parliament. In addition to the documentary evidence which forms the skeleton and main support of the study, there is also material drawn from interviews with a number of people connected with the work of the Expenditure Committee: members and ex-members of the Committees, Clerks of the House of Commons, civil servants and specialist advisers. A note on the numbers and types of interviews is provided in Appendix A at the end of the book. The interviews are a particularly valuable source for they supplement the analysis of documentary material by providing information about the relationships and working patterns of the sub-committees of the Expenditure Committee that could never be obtained in any other way. Not all members and ex-members of the Expenditure Committee have been interviewed, however, and no hard quantifiable data can be drawn from these interviews. Their value comes from the insights that they provided into Members' attitudes to their work on the Expenditure Committee, and as illustrations of patterns and trends. The case for the conclusions drawn in this study rests with material presented in the following chapters. It is hoped that this work may be a contribution to the understanding of how the British House of Commons actually works in practice, and that it may spark off further studies of a similar nature.

1 Parliament and Other Factors in the Determination of Patterns of Public Spending

'Parliaments are not only, what they always were, essential parts of our constitution, but essential parts of our administration too. They do not claim the executive power: No. But the executive power cannot be exercised without their annual concurrence.'

Henry St John (Viscount Bolinbroke), *The Spirit of Patriotism*, 1742.

Bolinbroke's classic statement of the need for Parliament to meet each year to vote the supply of funds to the Government describes the essence of the theory of Parliamentary control of public spending. According to this theory Government can be carried on only if Parliament agrees to provide it with money raised from the tax payer. Should Government come to Parliament with rash or extravagant notions likely to offend tax payers and voters, Parliament can refuse to grant supply to that Government. It must then either resign to allow some other Government to carry out the administration, or it must reformulate its spending plans so that these conform to Parliament's wishes. The implication is therefore that Parliament provides the ultimate check and control over public spending. The theory allotting to Parliament a central role in the process of determining levels and allocations of public spending is supposed to be one of the cornerstones of the British constitution.

The theory is comforting to the tax payer for the obvious reason that he likes to think that there is democratic control over the expenditure of the money that the Government takes from him. It is also a comfort to Parliamentarians who need to believe that they can exercise the power of the purse, since they have little else in the way of sanctions over recalcitrant Governments. This exercising of the power of the purse has to be done through Parliamentary procedures, the efficacy of which have been challenged in recent years by certain Members of the House of Commons—most notably by members of the Procedure Committee 1968–69[1]. The reforms of procedure recommended by that Committee were adopted by the House in the 1970s and their effect will be described in later sections of this book. For the moment the important thing to realise is that, when these reforms were proposed, the reformers did not question the basic assumption that Parliamentary control of public spending could be achieved. Acceptance of the traditional theory led them to conclude that the reason for the apparent loss of Parliamentary power over the public purse was a disjunction between Governmental and Parliamentary procedures. Once the procedures of Parliament were brought into line with the procedures of Government, so they believed, Parliament would recover its proper position in the constitution and in the process of influencing and determining public spending.

Unfortunately there are many reasons for doubting the validity of the theory in the context of Parliament in the late twentieth century. It was all very well for Bolinbroke to stress the role of Parliament as a check on the administration in a period when the Government spent little and provided few services. But in the late twentieth century most Governments spend a substantial proportion of a nation's resources. By the admission of the British Government itself public spending in 1976 took up some 60 per cent of national resources, and the national product is immeasurably greater now than it was two hundred years ago. The Government is the largest single employer in the country and its activities extend into almost every sphere of life. The process of administering and delivering its various services has become complex and diffuse. Such factors alone would make detailed scrutiny and control of public spending by an elected body of 635 members a very difficult task indeed.

There are those outside Parliament, among them economists and social theorists, viewing the processes of public spending, who do not allot Parliament the same potential position of influence over these processes. Whoever looks closely at the way in which decisions are made about how much Governments should spend will soon conclude that there are many factors involved apart from the need to satisfy Parliament. No one has yet attempted a full scale analysis of all the factors which together determine the levels and patterns of public spending, nor has the difficult task of evaluating the relative

[1] *Scrutiny of Public Expenditure and Adminstration*, H.C. 410 of 1968–69.

weight of Parliament against other factors been undertaken. But it is now clear that any evaluation of the success or otherwise of the new procedures adopted in the 1970s—especially the establishment of an Expenditure Committee to strengthen Parliament's role in the spending process—must take account of the fact that Parliament may be only one influence acting upon the Government when it comes to make its spending plans. As we shall show in this Chapter, too much has now been written about the process of public spending to allow anyone to maintain a crude and simplistic view of Parliament's power in this respect. The role of Parliament must be seen as one of *relative* power and influence, and must also be viewed in the context of the roles of other institutions and actors in the process. Only then can any judgement be made as to whether the new procedures have, or have not, enhanced its influence. Many academic studies— some of which are examined in more detail below—have been addressed to the question, 'What are the factors which in modern states determine the levels of public spending?' As a rule each study has a particular focus and emphasises one aspect of the process only. The many studies of the public spending processes have to be taken together to produce a list of the variables which seem to be of significance in determining spending. These variables include: the general attitudes of the public towards Government activities; the economic structures and particular pressures of the economy; the operations of the institutions and those working in them who are responsible for the actual expenditure of Government money; and the demands of interest groups and politicians for particular types of spending. Government and Parliament do not act alone. Whatever they decide about public spending is determined in part by forces beyond Westminster and Whitehall.

A powerful impression gained from reading the many works on public spending is that elected assemblies such as the British House of Commons play only a marginal role in the process. This impression arises probably because so many of those who have been interested in public spending have been economists rather than political scientists. They have, naturally, focussed their attention on the effects of economic forces rather than on the role of the political and administrative structures through which the economic forces are translated into policies and actions. Only in very recent years have a number of political scientists, first in the U.S.A. where 'Policy Studies' have become a popular branch of political science, and then in Britain, become interested in discovering and describing the forces that lie behind the patterns of public spending.[2] Interest in this subject, it seems, was only aroused when public spending became such a large proportion of the national income that its efficiency and fairness began to be questioned. Even so, studies of the political forces behind public spending decision are as yet sporadic and unsystematic.[3] K. Newton has observed that, given the practical and theoretical importance of public spending, it is odd that sociologists and political scientists have written relatively little about it. He suggests this may be in part due to the fact that public expenditure has been deemed to be a technical and economic matter best left to the experts. Only recently have some political scientists noticed that the expert economists themselves do not really understand what is going on.

The dominance of economists in the field of public spending studies means that many of the explanations for public spending patterns are related to the changing shape of the economy—especially to the development and transformations of the capitalist system from the nineteenth century onwards. Economic theories of expenditure are often broad and of a high level of generality. They purport to explain the total levels of public spending but do not try to explain the allocations of spending between different functions of Government. One of the first economists interested in the determinants of public spending was Adolf Wagner who traced the growth of public spending in the nineteenth century and attributed its expansion to three sources: (1) developments in regulatory services designed to control increasing economic specialisation and intercourse and their inevitable social frictions; (2) state participation in material production in order to supply and manage the vast amounts of new capital necessitated by promising ventures that were too risky and expensive for private capital (e.g. railroads, steam plants); and (3) an increase in the provision of social services whose benefits are not susceptible to equitable pricing in the market system (e.g. education, public health).[4] These variables are all broadly related to the development of the

[2] The extent to which policy studies have grown in recent years can be gauged from Hugh Heclo,'Review Article: Policy Analysis', *BJPS*, 2 (1972), 83–108; and Austin Ranney (ed.', *Political Science and Public Policy*, Markham, Chicago, 1968.

[3] Summaries of some of the works on the political factors determining public spending decisions appear in K. Newton, 'The Politics of Public Expenditure Studies', *PS*, XXV (March 1977), 122–7. See also Rudolf Klein, 'The Politics of Public Expenditure: American Theory and British Practice', *BJPS*, 6 (1976), 401–32.

[4] Adolf Wagner, *Grundlegung der politischen Oekonomie*, Leipzig, 1893. This section is based on comments by Ira Sharkansky, *The Politics of Taxing and Spending*, Bobbs-Merrill, Indianapolis & New York, pp. 147ff.

capitalist system which generates the need for Government expenditures. Marxist theorists of public expenditure determination likewise tie expansion of public spending to the capitalist system, although they suggest that governments are forced to increase their spending in order to prop up the capitalist system and to hoodwink the workers into believing that it is good for them.[5]

Wagner's theory was reviewed by Alan Peacock and Jack Wiseman[6] who, while accepting his general approach, suggest that an historical analysis of public expenditure changes in Britain shows that certain specific variables are closely correlated with changes in public spending. They found a strong correlation between times of crisis, especially wars, and rises in public spending. Public spending does not sink to former levels after the period of crisis is past because people become accustomed to higher levels of taxation. During normal times growth of public expenditure is kept in check by the level of taxation which is regarded as tolerable, but once people become accustomed to higher taxation in times of crisis they will sustain higher levels once the crisis is passed. The level of public spending is thus finally determined by the level of taxation found tolerable by the population. But the great rises in spending have come about as a result of crisis.

This conclusion was based on analysis of historical trends, and if the theory were accurate there would not have been a rapid or sharp rise in public spending during the 1960s and 1970s in any country which did not face a crisis or war. The great rise in British public spending in these peacetime years since Peacock and Wiseman published their work throws doubt on their analysis of the causes of increased public spending, although their claims that tolerable levels of taxation determine the upper limits are supported by other evidence. It is notable that the 'revisionist' brand of Labour Party ideology in mid-1977 is based precisely on the point that taxation limits restrict the future expansion of public expenditure.[7]

Explanations for the rise in public spending in Britain between 1958 and 1977 must take account of more variables, some subtle in operation, and unlike Peacock and Wiseman's crisis thesis not easily

---

[5] James O'Connor, *The Fiscal Crisis of the State*, St Martin's Press, New York, 1973. See also Ian Gough, 'State Expenditure in Advanced Capitalism', *New Left Review*, 92 (1975), 53–92.

[6] Alan Peacock and Jack Wiseman, *The Growth of Public Expenditure in the United Kingdom, 1890–1955*, Allen and Unwin, London, 1961.

[7] William Rodgers, Crosland Memorial Lecture. Partially reprinted as an article in *The Sunday Times*, 22 May 1977.

amenable to measurement and correlation. Among the reasons suggested for the rapid growth of public spending in Britian after 1958 were a change in political philosophy towards greater reliance on collective provision of goods and services; a change in methods of financing local government; attempts to control public expenditure in the Treasury through the use of new management and accounting techniques; and the aggregate result of individual demands for better services from constituency-oriented Members of Parliament.[8] The final limits of public expenditure, according to this analysis, may not be simply the tolerable level of taxation but the balance of political philosophy between freedom of choice and government direction and control which the tolerated level of taxation reflects. It seems likely from the retrenching statements by some members of the Labour Government (for example, William Rogers in his Crosland Memorial Lecture and even Denis Healey in his 1977 Budget statements) in the years 1976 and 1977 that the expansion of public spending from 1958 had by the mid-1970s already overshot tolerable levels of taxation.

The idea that legislative outputs reflect the values held by society is not a new one. A. V. Dicey in *Law and Opinion in England*, first published in 1905, showed how general values changed during the nineteenth century from individualism towards greater appreciation of collective effort and how these changes of opinion were responsible for legislation for collective provision of goods and services. K. Galbraith in *The Affluent Society* also discussed the connection between societal values and legislative output. He argued that public spending attitudes in the United States of America did not support a high level of public spending; the result was, as he put it, 'private affluence and public squalor'. He suggested that changes in economic structure had led to changes in the need for public as opposed to private spending, but that in the United States the political system had not responded to the changing needs of society, in part since public attitudes did not recognise these new needs. How much public spending would in practice satisfy Galbraith is not clear. If we look at the actual figures for public spending in the United States, we find that there as in other Western nations public spending has expanded year by year. It is clear that, in spite of what he said of the United States in the 1960s, a general attitude has prevailed in all Western nations since World War II that Government should provide for the

[8] Cedric Sandford and Paul Dean, 'Public Expenditure: Why it has Grown', *The Banker*, April 1970. Cedric Sandford and Ann Robinson, 'Public Spending', *The Banker*, November 1975.

well-being of the people. The 'Welfare State' which has developed in response to these attitudes has only been checked after 30 years of popularity when in the 1970s economic growth—the lynch pin of the expansion of public services—declined, thus raising the question of whether public spending could continue to expand at the expense of private consumption. In some countries the check has been expressed in new political parties such as the Danish anti-tax party, in others by a subtle change of attitudes in existing parties.

The broad theories of public expenditure determination based on changes in the structure of the economy or in the pattern of attitudes can only, at best, explain shifts in the total level of public spending. They do not explain the levels of spending on individual functions of Government. Indeed they are so broad that they may not even be capable of explaining fully the precise levels of public expenditure that may occur. It has been suggested that other factors, technical in nature, can cause the actual level of public expenditure to rise above that which is desired by the populace and required to satisfy the needs of the economy. In Britain the public expenditure level prevailing in the late 1970s is quite different from those levels desired by the population and planned for by politicians and bureaucrats. One of the most significant factors leading to the rise in public expenditure in Britain from 1961 was an unexpected technical effect of the introduction of a system designed to allow the Cabinet to make more rational decisions about future public spending. Each year as the five-year forward plans for spending were drawn up, the future size of programmes was related to Treasury forecasts of the growth of available resources in the economy. The Cabinet made its decisions about the future shape of programmes in the light of the expected growth in the economy. In practice Treasury forecasts of economic growth always turned out too optimistic. Led by such forecasts into a false sense of reassurance respecting income, Governments initiated new programmes and expanded existing ones. If, however, levels of spending are determined in the light of particular expectations of future economic growth and these expectations are not fulfilled, the percentage of the economic resources taken up by public expenditure will rise automatically. A Government facing lower rates of actual economic growth than it has expected must prune or hold back on public expenditure if it does not want to alter the balance in the economy between public and private sectors. Most British Governments have found it extremely difficult to cut or hold back on public spending plans. The result has been that in almost every year since 1961 when the Public Expenditure Survey Committee (PESC) was established public expenditure has pre-empted a higher proportion of the national resources than the Cabinet intended. Thus for almost accidental reasons the actual level of public spending in Britain has been substantially different from the level planned by politicians.

A slightly more refined approach to the determinants of public spending is found in the work of Richard Musgrave, who suggests that it is not possible to explain the whole range of public expenditure by one set of explanations. He has examined the goals desired by the politicians and bureaucrats who shape budgets. In his view public expenditure is divided into different categories serving different goals. Expenditure can be used for public capital formation, for public consumption of goods and services, and for transfer payments which result ultimately in some form of private consumption. Different variables may be needed to explain the levels of spending in the different categories.[9] He has also suggested that the different branches of the budget can be seen to perform different functions in the economy and society.[10]

Before examining what Musgrave and others have to say about the making of budgets and the functions that they perform it is important to make it clear just what is meant by the term budget. This term has different meanings in different countries, and indeed in different contexts and different times within the same country. In many countries the budget is the annual statement produced by a Government to indicate how much it is going to spend in the forthcoming year and how much it is expecting to receive in income from taxation and other sources.[11] In Britain the budget refers to the annual (or sometimes more frequent) statement by the Chancellor of the Exchequer about Government revenue. It also provides an occasion for discussion of general economic policy. In the United States the term budget at Federal Government level refers to the President's annual statement of intended expenditures. However, in Britain, as in other countries, academics and commentators when referring to the 'budgetary process' most commonly mean both taxing and spending, although some mean the process of determining spending alone. Musgrave is concerned with both sides of the financial equation.

[9] Richard Musgrave, *Fiscal Systems*, McGraw Hill, New York, 1969.
[10] Richard Musgrave, 'A Multiple Theory of Budget Determination', *Finanzarchiv*, 1957, Vol., 333–43.
[11] For a discussion of the difficulties of defining the term budget see David Coombes (ed.), *The Power of the Purse: The Role of European Parliaments in Budgetary Decisions*, Allen and Unwin/PEP, London, 1976, p. 15, pp. 164–5 and p. 179.

Firstly in the budgetary process, says Musgrave, there is the service branch which has to decide which public wants should be satisfied, how much should be spent on them, and who should bear the cost. This requires budget makers to draw a distinction between public and private goods. A second function of budgets is concerned with the ability to pay for the services provided and can be thought of as a distributive or a 'Robin Hood' function. Budget makers have to take this function into account. Finally, budgets are used as an instrument for stabilisation of the economy, to maintain an appropriate level of aggregate demand and to regulate inflationary and deflationary tendencies. Public spending thus being arranged by the budget makers with these various functions in mind, budgets do not simply reflect the wants and needs of society but allocate the liability to pay for these wants and correct undesirable economic fluctuations. Musgrave's view of the budgetary process is that the technical factors required to manage the economy intervene between the values of society and the legislative output of budgetary dispositions, so that the total level of public spending is not a precise reflection of societal attitudes.

Few of the economists who are concerned with the relationship between economic variables and public spending say very much about the specific role of the various political institutions through which a budget has to pass. It is as though, for the economist viewing the expenditure process, the political institutions are mere filters through which economic forces are automatically translated into policies and as though these filters have little if any effect upon the outcomes. Only technical factors seem to intervene to upset the exact relationship between economic forces and public spending. Musgrave does at least offer some indication of factors which might be in the minds of budget makers and in so doing introduces a consideration of political behaviour into the expenditure equation, but he only looks at the broad intentions of budget makers, not at their specific attitudes and behaviour. Davis, Dempster and Wildavsky go further than Musgrave in making studies of the actual behaviour of administrators and legislators who take part in the budgetary process. Their enquiries reveal that budget makers approach their task incrementally.[12] Budgets are almost never actively reviewed as a whole in the sense of considering at one time the value of all existing programmes and comparing these with all possible alternatives. Instead

[12] Otto Davis, N. A. H. Dempster and Aaron Wildavsky, 'A Theory of the Budgetary Process', *APSR*, lx (September 1966), 529–47.

each year's budget is based upon last year's budget with incremental changes. The model of budget determination developed by these authors is described by them as 'stochastic rather than deterministic'. The budgetary process is stable over a period of time and such changes as are made take place step by step. Thus it becomes possible to estimate future changes in budgets in relation to past patterns of spending, for the variations will be relatively small from year to year. The general pattern can, however, be disturbed by outside events. There may be changes of Government, and crises may provide 'random shocks' to an otherwise stable, incremental process of public spending decision making. Unless such exceptional events cause the system to vary widely, the major determinant of the size of next year's budget will be that of last year's.[13]

The incremental model of public spending decision making is based largely upon empirical studies of administrative and elite behaviour. It asserts that the reasons for the incremental or stepwise approach to budget making can be sought in the processes and structural rules by which the spending plans are formulated and in the behaviour and roles played by the individuals who work that process. A recent study uses this model to analyse the British public spending process. Hugh Heclo and Aaron Wildavsky suggest that the need to maintain good working relationships between the inhabitants of the 'public expenditure community'—which is basically the civil servants of the Treasury and the departmental finance officers—results in a process of give and take and bargaining over expenditure changes. No administrators or Ministers like to see their departments suffer from cut backs and this gives them an impetus to carry forward existing programmes without radical re-evaluation. As in the United States budgets are not re-established from the base upwards each year. Changes in public spending tend not to be radical but to be marginal incremental changes which hurt no one's feelings and disturb no established communities.

Recent published diaries, biographies and memoirs of British Cabinet members suggest that, although the general process is incremental, the precise marginal changes made to budgets are determined by the personalities and abilities of individual politicians

---

[13] This particular theory of budget determination has been criticised by R. Greenwood, C. R. Hinings and S. Ranson, for its failure to explain the variations in English local government budgets. See 'Budgetary Processes in English Local Government', *Political Studies*, xxv (March 1977), 25–47. They do not however reject the finding that budgets are *mainly* based on previous budgets.

pushing their own departmental cases in Cabinet discussions.[14] The over-all thrust of studies of administration and elite behaviour in the budgetary process supports the theory of the 'unseen hand' as the explanation for the patterns of public spending. Roland N. McKeen[15] traces the theory of the unseen hand to the work of C. E. Lindblom,[16] who has concluded that budgetary decisions are made by mutual adjustment between decision makers. Bargaining between the actors is the means whereby the adjustments are made. Administrators do not, in Lindblom's view, make clear definitions of goals and then devise the most effective means of achieving them. Neither do they have sufficient information to allow complete evaluation of all possible alternatives which could be selected. Politicians and administrators therefore 'muddle through' when making their policy and budgetary decisions taking each other's position into account. The levels and patterns of spending reached by the 'unseen hand' may be rational in terms of the limited goals and knowledge of the actors and their need to adjust to each other's demands. But they may be very different from decisions made under a system of rational planning.[17]

A variation on the bureaucratic behaviour model of budget making is provided by the economist William A. Niskanen. Niskanen believes that bureaucrats themselves are the main determinators of budgets.[18] He defines bureaucrats as those who work in non-profit making organisations financed by grants. This class of persons has different motives from people working in profit making organisations because the incentives and constraints which operate on the one class do not operate on the other. Bureaucrats do not have to show a profit and loss account on their operations; their main aims are neither to satisfy

[14] Hugh Heclo and Aaron Wildavsky make this point in *The Private Government of Public Spending*, Macmillan, London, 1974. It is confirmed by several passages in Richard Crossman, *Diaries of a Cabinet Minister*, Hamish Hamilton & Cape, London, (1975–76), and in numerous newspaper reports of Cabinet discussions of the public spending cuts made in the 1975–77 period.

[15] Roland N. McKeen, *Public Spending*, McGraw Hill, New York, 1969.

[16] Charles E. Lindblom, 'The Science of "Muddling Through"', *Public Administration*, xix, (Spring 1969), 79–88; also David Braybrooke and Charles Lindblom, *A Strategy of Decision: Policy Evaluation as a Social Process*, Macmillan, London, 1963, and Charles Lindblom, *The Intelligence of Democracy*, Macmillan, London, 1965.

[17] Although Lindblom considers that the methods of decision making he describes are rational, that is not the view of other observers. For criticisms of Lindblom, see T. Lowi, *The End of Liberalism*, Norton, New York, 1969, and Charles T. Schultze, *The Politics and Economics of Public Spending*, Brookings, Washington D.C., 1968.

[18] William A. Niskanen, *Bureaucracy and Representative Government*, Aldine–Atherton, New York, 1971. See also Niskanen, *Bureaucracy: Servant or Master?*, Hobart Paperback, The Institute for Economic Affairs, London, 1973.

their customers nor to ensure that their sponsors get the best value for money. They find instead that their satisfaction comes from maximising their own personal utility. This is done by maximising the budgets of the bureaux in which they work because:

> Among the several variables that may enter the bureaucrats' motives are: salary, perquisites of the office, public reputation, power, patronage, output of the bureau, ease of making changes, and ease of managing the bureau. All except the last two are a positive function of the total *budget* of the bureau during the bureaucrat's tenure.[19]

Many forces acting together produce the budget maximising behaviour—even if the bureaucrats themselves see their role as one of Weberian servants of their political masters. Pressures come from all sides, even from other employees who see in larger budgets more opportunities for promotion and more job security. Are there any controls over these pressures by bureaucrats to maximise their budgets? Niskanen says of legislative oversight:

> One point, however, is not generally understood: both the executive and the legislative officers reviewing the bureau fully expect the bureaucrat to propose aggressively more activities and higher budgets. Indeed, they would not otherwise know how to perform their review role.[20]

The real problem facing legislatures in attempting to provide oversight of bureaucratic spending is that they have no alternative sources of information with which to compare the bureau's own estimates of costs —for many of the functions performed by public bureaux are not performed by any comparable private profit making organisations. Niskanen points out, moreover, that the detailed review of a bureau's proposed budget is usually performed by a specialised legislative committee which is dominated by representatives of groups in the population with relatively high demands for the services of the bureaux. Thus the political benefits are visible to the advocates of programmes but the political costs—in terms of taxes—are less visible as they are borne by the whole polity. Advocacy of spending programmes tends to be concentrated and carefully argued whereas opposition is diffused. As a result all bureaux are too large and spend

---

[19] Niskanen, *Bureaucracy: Servant or Master*, p. 22.
[20] *Bureaucracy: Servant or Master*, p. 25. Here Niskanen quotes Aaron Wildavsky, *The Politics of the Budgetary Process*, and the review role referred to here is that of the United States Congress.

more than they need to. Public expenditure grows because the pressures from the bureaucracy combine with the pressures from the political system for the supply of services to make government budgets larger than the size which would be produced if demand and supply of the system were to reach equilibrium.

Studies of bureaucratic behaviour are generally, like Wildavsky's and Niskanen's work, based on the American experience. But both of these models have some relevance for Britain. Wildavsky and Heclo tested the incremental behaviour model of decision making in their book on British expenditure decision making, *The Private Government of Public Spending*. They did not find that British bureaucrats behaved in a manner fundamentally different from that of their American counterparts. There has been no empirical test of the Niskanen model although his ideas were published in the United Kingdom by the Institute for Economic Affairs in a pamphlet that also contained comments on his model from British political scientists and politicians. Only one of these, Douglas Houghton, in a comment entitled 'Fundamental UK–US differences', suggested that the British form of bureaucracy was so different from the American form that Niskanen's model was of dubious utility[21] in the British context.

Theories of public spending determination which focus on administrative or elite behaviour generally give scant consideration to political variables such as the political pressures on the decision makers. According to administrative theories decision makers live in a world of their own, hermetically sealed off from contamination by the demands of the populace. There may be some truth in the assumption that budget makers face few political constraints on their behaviour, but most of those employed in the higher ranks of administration and in Cabinet posts do of necessity have to take some account of views expressed elsewhere in the political system, for example the political parties, pressure groups, and legislatures. Unfortunately the political dimension of the public expenditure process remains relatively little explored and there are no systematic studies which chart the effects of these variables on the size of budgets. Almost all of the studies of the political effects on public expenditures decisions that have so far been undertaken have been concerned with state expenditures in the U.S.A. Most have attempted to measure the effect of all political variables together, or the effect of party competition, in comparison with the effects of socio-economic variables in determining expenditures. Most of these studies have shown that political variables have less measurable effect

[21] Niskanen, *Bureaucracy: Servant or Master*, comment by Douglas Houghton, pp. 67–74.

upon the shape of budgets than do socio-economic variables. The studies have, however, been criticised on grounds of their methodology and because state politicians draw up their budgets under political constraints not applicable in the national context.[22] None of these studies lists all possible political variables, let alone tries to measure their relative effects. One economist, Albert Breton, has gone so far in his theory of public spending to include all these political factors in his general equation. This is in its way a great advance. The trouble with his particular approach is that while he includes all the variables, he does not weigh the relative effects and importance of each.[23]

A few economists have addressed themselves to the role of individual political variables in the public spending process while not tying these with a general theory. It is interesting that Anthony Downs, who has addressed himself to the connection between political parties and election promises on the one hand and public spending on the other, has come to a completely different conclusion regarding the size of budgets from one reached by Niskanen who concentrated on bureaucrats alone. In several of his works Downs has used economic methods of analysis to try to explain the operation of politics. He maintains that political parties in a democratic system are in competition for votes and try to obtain as many votes as are necessary to be elected and form a Government. Parties compete for votes by promising to provide services for the population. This of course entails expenditure of public funds. There are limits on the number of promises which a party can reasonably make to the electorate in order to obtain votes because the electorate is aware that publicly provided goods and services have to paid for out of taxation.

[22] Examples of attempts to measure the effects of political and other variables in determining public spending include: R. E. Dawson and J. A. Robinson, 'Inter-party Competition, Economic Variables and Welfare Policies in the American States', *Journal of Politics*, 25 (1963), 265–89; Charles F. Cnudde and D. McCrone, 'Party Competition and Welfare Policies in the American States', *APSR*, 63 (1969), 858–66; Richard I. Hofferbert, 'The Relation between Public Policy and some Structural and Environmental Variables in the American States', *APSR*, 60 (1966), 73–82; Thomas Dye, *Politics, Economics and the Public*, Rand McNally, Chicago, 1966; Ira Sharkansky and R. I. Hofferbert, 'Dimensions of State Politics, Economics and Public Policy', *APSR*, 63 (1969), 867–79; Brian R. Fry and Richard F. Winters, 'The Politics of Redistribution', *APSR*, 64 (1970), 508–22; Bernard H. Booms and James R. Halldorson, 'The Politics of Redistribution: a Reformulation', *APSR*, 67 (1973), 924–33; Gary L. Tomkins, 'A Causal Model of State Welfare Expenditures', *Journal of Politics*, 37 (1975), 392–416. For a criticism of this literature see James Anderson, *Public Policy Making*, Nelson, London, 1975.

[23] Albert Breton, *The Economic Theory of Representative Government*, Macmillan, London, 1975.

Downs believes that taxation is relatively visible to the voter who sees his annual bill and recognises it as a burden imposed by Government. On the other hand a number of the goods and services promised to the electorate are relatively visible to the voter. He knows that he must pay his tax demand but he may never have been ill and may have no children to be educated. Thus he may feel that he is paying something for nothing. On these assumptions about the relative visibility of costs and benefits of public spending to the voter Downs concludes that the total of public spending is always smaller in a democracy than it would be if the real needs of the public were to be met. Politicians could provide limitless services but are checked by fear of electoral unpopularity if they produce policies resulting in increased taxation.[24]

Material on the role of pressure groups in the spending process is scattered and incoherent because students of pressure group politics nearly always limit their detailed examination to the operation of individual groups rather than provide a general theory of pressure group activities in relation to spending. Only Mancur Olson offers any clue to the general importance of pressure groups in the distribution of public goods. He relates the size of these groups to their degree of success in obtaining collective goods and says furthermore that the larger the group the farther it will fall short of providing the optimal amount of a collective good for its members. Groups become proportionately less efficient as they get larger. Their costs of communication, bargaining, and formal organisation rise. These costs tend to increase relative to the amount of public goods that can be obtained. So a sensible approach for a pressure group wishing to maximise its share of public goods is to remain as small in size and as specific in its demands as possible.[25]

Political scientists have paid much more attention to the role of legislatures in the public spending process than they have to the influences of other variables.[26] Most of their findings confirm the

---

[24] A. Downs, *An Economic Theory of Democracy*, Harper and Row, New York, 1957. Also A. Downs, 'Why the Government Budget is too Small in a Democracy', *World Politics*, July 1960, pp. 541–63. For a criticism of his assumptions of the relative visibility of taxation and expenditure, see Rudolf Klein, 'The Politics of Public Expenditure', *BJPS*, 6 (1976), 401–32.

[25] Mancur Olson, *The Logic of Collective Action: Public Goods and the Theory of Groups*, Harvard Economic Studies, Harvard University Press, Cambridge, Mass., 1965.

[26] Most of the literature charting the role of legislatures in the public spending process is concerned to describe and evaluate the processes and procedures of control. Few studies examine the role of legislatures relative to other variables in the expenditure determination equation. For the British legislature's role, see Basil

economists' view that legislatures are relatively insignificant in the determination of public spending. However, the reasons behind the findings are separate from the economists' reasons. Those political scientists who have examined the role of legislatures in the budgetary process constantly reiterate that, as public spending has risen in the twentieth century, so the democratic political structures have had their procedures subtly altered to accommodate governmentally and bureaucratically determined budgets. Large and complicated budgets, if subject to detailed legislative scrutiny, give scope for obstruction. Thus governments must either find ways to speed them through the legislature or spend money in ways which obviate the need for regular legislative oversight.

Many countries have in recent years altered the rules of budgetary process to circumvent the necessity for political interference with the normal flow of spending. The new rules ensure that the scope for legislative influence is diminished. Procedural alterations have included a rise in spending by government agencies not directly subject to legislative oversight such as the British local authorities which by 1975 accounted for one-third of all public spending in the United Kingdom, and the passage of legislation committing the Government to long term spending such as the provision of pensions or involving it in open-ended financial commitments like unemployment benefits. Studies of the U.S.A. and of many European countries show that such developments in the budgetary process are commonplace. According to Murray L. Wiedenbaum the result of these developments in the U.S.A. is that only about half the total public expenditure can now be classified as 'relatively controllable' by the democratic

---

Chubb, *The Control of Public Expenditure*, Clarendon Press, Oxford, 1952; Paul Einzig, *The Control of the Purse*, London, 1959; Nevil Johnson, *Parliament and Administration: The Estimates Committee 1945–65*, Allen and Unwin, London, 1966; Gordon Reid, *The Politics of Financial Control*, Hutchinson, London, 1966; and Ann Robinson, 'The House of Commons and Public Expenditure', in S. A. Walkland and Michael Ryle (eds), *The Commons in the Seventies*, Fontana, London, 1977. David Coombes *et al.*, *The Power of the Purse*, Allen and Unwin/PEP, London, 1976 describes the processes in the Federal Republic of Germany, France, Britain, Italy, the Netherlands and Switzerland. Guy Lord, *The French Budgetary Process*, Berkeley, California, 1973, gives more detail on France than the Coombes' volume. There are a great many books on the U.S. Congress that examine the budgetary process among other procedures but the study of the Appropriations process by Richard Fenno, *The Power of the Purse*, Little Brown, Boston, 1966, remains a classic. A useful discussion of the new Congressional Budget process is found in John H. Ellwood and James A. Thurber, 'The New Congressional Budget Process: the Hows and Whys of House–Senate Differences', in Lawrence C. Doad and Bruce I. Oppenheim (eds), *Congress Reconsidered*, Praeger, New York, 1977.

institutions.[27] An American Government estimate suggests an even more dramatic picture with about 75 per cent of the U.S. Federal Budget being 'relatively uncontrollable under existing law'.[28] Institutional blocks on legislative control over budgets in the U.S.A. include: trust funds whereby such items as social insurance are controlled under permanent legislation and are not subject to annual scrutiny (in 1969 such funds accounted for 27 per cent of the U.S. Federal budget); permanent and indefinite authorisations for spending on items such as the national debt (accounting for some 10 per cent of the Federal budget); and other fixed charges and partially completed projects (adding up to another 10 per cent). All these items together make up such a large proportion of the Federal budget that Congress has little elbow room to adjust the plans presented to it by the President.

Guy Lord has described a similar pattern of institutional development in France.[29] A division is made in the French budgetary process between old and new programmes. This distinction is intitutionalised in the budgetary process under the Organic Law of the Fifth Republic. The effect of the Organic Law is that ongoing programmes cannot, in effect, be subject to alteration by the National Assembly. Moreover, the amount of spending in France which falls outside the annual budget as presented to the Assembly is considerable and includes such items as the universities, hospitals, museums, nationalised industries and semi-public bodies such as those controlling social insurance funds. These extra-budgetary items further reduce the opportunities for democratic control over spending plans of the Government.

A similar pattern of institutional development has occurred in Britain. In particular spending by local authorities now accounts for about one third of all public spending and has expanded more rapidly than has spending by Central Government departments. From 1964 to 1974 local government spending as a percentage of Gross

---

[27] Murray L. Weidenbaum, 'Institutional Obstacles to Reallocating Government Expenditures', in Robert H. Haveman and Julius Margolis (eds), *Public Expenditure and Policy Analysis*, Markham Publishing Co., Chicago, 1970; and 'On the Effectiveness of Congressional Control of the Public Purse', *National Tax Journal*, December 1965. For European countries see David Coombes (ed.), *The Power of the Purse*. P. E. P., Allen and Unwin, London, 1975.

[28] John H. Ellwood and James A. Thurber, 'The New Congressional Budget Process: the Hows and Whys of House–Senate Differences', in Lawrence C. Doad and Bruce I. Oppenheim, *Congress Reconsidered*, Praeger, New York, 1977, p. 166. Their estimate is taken from *The Budget of the United States Government*, Fiscal *Year 1977*, Government Printing Office, Washington D.C., 1977, pp. 6–10

[29] Guy Lord, *The French Budgetary Process*, University of California Press, Berkeley, California, 1973.

National Product rose by 40 per cent while Central Government spending rose by 25 per cent in the same period.[30] Yet the opportunities for Parliament to consider this sizeable and growing chunk of the public sector are virtually non-existent. Devolution in Scotland and Wales, should it come about, would further reduce those sections of public spending which are subject to annual scrutiny by the House of Commons. Unlike the French Assembly, the British House of Commons is constrained by no constitutional rules limiting its competence to scrutinise budgets—it has simply given away its rights by creating a loose adminstrative structure to process the mass of public provision and services.

Central and Local Government Spending 1964–74

	Percentage of GNP			Percentage of Total Public Expenditure		
Years	Central	Local	Combined	Central	Local	Combined
1964	28.3	12.3	40.6	69.7	30.3	100
1965	29.3	13.0	42.2	69.3	30.7	100
1966	29.9	13.4	43.3	69.1	30.9	100
1967	33.0	14.4	47.4	69.6	30.4	100
1968	34.1	14.6	48.7	70.0	30.0	100
1969	33.0	14.8	47.8	69.1	30.9	100
1970	32.4	15.2	47.6	68.1	31.9	100
1971	32.5	14.9	47.4	68.7	31.3	100
1972	32.8	15.3	48.1	68.2	31.8	100
1973	31.3	16.2	47.4	65.9	34.1	100
1974	35.4	17.1	52.5	67.4	32.6	100

Notes: The figures exclude grants from central to local government and interest on loans from central government.
Source: National Income and Expenditure 1964–74, tables 1 and 52, HMSO 1975.

It is clear that Governments have so manipulated and adjusted the budgetary processes of modern states that elected assembles would find much had escaped their net even if they wished to exert detailed control. But procedural changes are not the only reason behind legislative weakness. Procedures are living entities shaped and formed by the people who operate them. Even if the procedural rules allow a legislature a reasonable degree of influence, there is no guarantee that members of the legislature will use the rules to best advantage. The behaviour of parliamentarians is as important a factor in their relatively weak position in regard to public spending as are the procedural constraints placed upon them. Studies of the budgetary

[30] See Cedric Sandford and Ann Robinson, 'Public Spending' *The Banker*, November 1975, table 5, p. 1246.

process in the United States show that even the relatively strong Congress only makes marginal changes to the President's spending plans. One reason for this is that a democratic system encourages close links between the elected Congressman and his local constituency and the interest groups that have supported his candidature. These links tend to produce demands for increased spending on individual and local items serving to encourage Government departments in their spending plans and bolster up the pressures towards large budgets which come from the bureaucrats. The local and particular orientations of Congressmen moreover discourage them from radical evaluation of spending plans and from consideration of either the total desired levels of expenditure or the relative allocations of the total among competing functions of Government. So many political scientists have described the atomistic approach to policy making within the Congress that it would take pages of footnotes to list them all. Ernest Griffith sums up the general view concisely:

> Congressmen are responsible to their districts and states. This gives them an undue or distorted concern as to the location of navy bases, army camps, airfields—not to mention the awarding of contracts to firms who are their constituents.[31]

The links between Congressmen and their constituents affect their attitude to their work on the comittees which make budget decisions.

> I wanted Interior because I came from a Western state and the Committee deals with matters like dams, parks, recreation, mines, public lands—all especially important to the so-called public lands states. Everything I can get from the Committee—big dams, mining, outdoor recreation, parks—helps me back home.[32]

Differences between Congressmen in committees and on the floor of the House are settled by bargaining and trade-offs. The result of the attitude and behaviour of the Congressmen is that they do not make a clear evaluation of either the total level of public spending or the relative allocations between competing functions of Government.

One of the most articulate critics of the Congressional role in public spending is Senator William Proxmire who has said: 'In the Congress ... there is very little explicit consideration of program objectives or tradeoffs, of alternative means of attaining objectives. ...

---

[31] Ernest S. Griffith, *Congress: Its Contemporary Role*, 4th edn., New York University Press, 1967, p. 195.

[32] Interview with a Congressman in Richard Fenno, *Congressmen in Committees*, Little Brown, Boston, 1973, pp. 139–40. See also the same author's study of the Appropriations Process in *The Power of the Purse*, Little Brown, Boston, 1966.

Congress does not really give the Budget a meaningful review because it fails to ask the right questions.'[33] The executive presents only one budget to the Congress and does not give quantitative information on the benefits or costs of even its own proposals. Congressmen have little interest in or patience for careful deliberation on budgetary matters. Congress does not have enough staff to evaluate the executive's program, and the organisation and structure of the Appropriations Committee where each sub-committee deals with particular portion of the budget means that

> there is pressure to put on these sub-committees men who have a particular interest in, and benefit from that type of spending and they like to see 'their' budget rise. The whole leads to a substantial degree of mutuality of interests between the executive staff and those on legislative branch committees.[34]

Proxmire's criticisms were made before the passage of the 1974 reforms, which established firstly the House and Senate Budget Committees to co-ordinate the Congressional response to the President's budget, and secondly the Congressional Budget Office with its large staff to feed the Budget Committees with information on the state of the economy, on alternative budgets and costs. Since the introduction of this new machinery, budgets have indeed been subject to greater Congressional influence. The true test of this machinery has yet to come, however, for Congress has in recent years faced a weakened Presidency. Only when it confronts a President who knows his mind and is prepared to stick to his position will the effectiveness of the reforms become known. It has been suggested that the final effect of the 1974 reforms might, ironically, be to move the Congressional system closer to the British 'responsible party' model of Government.[35] For a fragmented approach to the President's budget has been replaced by a system which requires the development of a firm party line on the over-all size and scope of the expenditure plans.

Just as complaints of Congressional weakness with respect to the Government's budget plans were common in the late 1960s and early 1970s, so were similar complaints about the British House of Commons. Commentators suggested that the British Parliament had

[33] Senator William Proxmire, 'P.P.B., The Agencies and Congress', in Robert H. Haveman and Julius Margolis (eds), *Public Expenditure and Policy Analysis*, Rand, Chicago, p. 414. See also William Proxmire, *Can Congress Control Spending?* American Enterprise Institute, Washington D.C., 1973.

[34] Proxmire, 'P.P.B., The Agencies and Congress', p. 416.

[35] Ellwood and Thurber, 'The New Congressional Budget Process', p. 187.

lost its actual ability to control public spending even though the theory of parliamentary control remained. The lack of control over money weakened the role of Parliament in the whole political system. Andrew Hill and Anthony Whichelow stated in *What's Wrong with Parliament:* 'The control of the nation's money is at the heart of our parliamentary system. It is right that we should turn to consider it first, for it may be that Parliament is suffering from heart trouble.'[36] In their view the Government's spending plans were not greatly affected by the scrutiny of them made in the House of Commons:

> We have noticed how, in theory, the House spends a great deal of its time each year in examining the individual Estimates of expenditure which the Government have laid before it. To qualify that impression of a vigilant, suspicious House, we must now notice that this long-drawn out examination, year after year, results in no economies at all. It is indeed more than forty years since the House forced the Government to reduce an estimate—and then it was a proposal concerning Members' own travelling allowances that they were so bold as to reject. Two years earlier (in 1919) in another headstrong flurry of economy, the House had thrown out an Estimate designed to provide a second bathroom in the Lord Chancellor's residence. These are the only two occasions on which the Government's plans of Expenditure, as expressed in the Estimate, have been thwarted by a parsimonious House since the First World War.[37]

Much was said in Britain in the 1960s about the relatively small amount of influence of the House of Commons over the Government's spending plans. Almost every commentator seemed to believe that the defects could be remedied by new procedures. Critics of the role of the House were mesmerised by their adherence to traditional views of the British Constitution and by their belief in procedural change:

> One thing stands out clearly with hindsight (although some of us predicted it) which is that the main weakness of the Parliamentary reform movement is that it did not presuppose political change, without which its innovations have been weakened almost to the point of impotence. When one looks at the arguments of the reformers one is constantly struck by how unpolitical they were, apparently unaware of the wider political context in which reforms would have to operate.[38]

[36] Andrew Hill and Anthony Whichelow, *What's Wrong with Parliament?* Penguin, London, 1964, pp. 15–16.

[37] Andrew Hill and Anthony Whichelow, *op. cit.*, p. 18.

[38] S. A. Walkland, 'Whither the Commons?', in S. A. Walkland and Michael Ryle (eds), *The Commons in the Seventies*, Fontana, London, 1977, p. 243.

But as we have shown in this chapter the traditional theory of parliamentary control of public spending must be considered in the light of all the other factors which together shape the decisions about spending. Even with the best of all possible procedures Parliament alone could not control public spending. There are too many other pressures coming from the economic and political system when a Government spends as much as half of the annual national income. These create structural impediments to realisation of the reformers' hopes for a more effective House of Commons.

There are also behavioural impediments to an effective House. Many political scientists from the 1950s onwards have studied the behaviour of members of the U.S. Congress and the resultant knowledge of behaviour has provided some idea of the likely consequences of procedural change in the legislature. But when the reformers of the 1960s in Britain clamoured for a more effective House of Commons, almost nothing was heard about the attitudes, motivations, and behaviour of those members of that House who would be called upon to operate the new procedures. Indeed practically nothing was known about the behaviour of members of the British House of Commons. The behavioural approach was popular in the U.S.A. by then but had not found any favour in Britain. This was an outstanding defect, for any understanding of the effectiveness of changes in procedure could not be complete without an appreciation of how members might react to the new procedures. In general terms, therefore, new procedures may be proposed and instituted, but procedural devices are shaped eventually by the men who use them. The influence of the House of Commons over public spending is certainly constrained by structural factors and by procedural rules, but it is also determined by the attitudes, motivation, and behaviour of the members, It is up to them whether they make best use of the opportunities with which they are provided, even if these offer limited influence rather than absolute power.

How the Members of Parliament have used the new opportunities presented to them by the institution of annual debates on Public Expenditure White Papers and by the establishment of an Expenditure Committee forms the substance of the following chapters. Any evaluation of the success or failure of these new devices must, however, take into account the constraints upon the ability of the House of Commons to exercise political influence or power over Governments in respect of public spending. It must be clear from the foregoing pages that the greatest constraint upon the House of Commons comes from the number of different factors at work in the determination of public spending levels and patterns. Even the Government, which is often thought to be the greatest constraint on House of Commons power, is subject to many influences when it comes to make its public spending decisions. In this respect Britain is no different from any other economically developed country that chooses to spend the greater part of its wealth in the public domain. Those who proposed reforms in the procedure of the House of Commons in the 1960s to remedy its perceived deficiencies paid insufficient attention to the wider context of public expenditure decision making. Yet in evaluating the success or otherwise of the new procedures, the relative position of Government and Parliament against other factors must constantly be borne in mind if any realistic conclusions are to be drawn respecting the extent to which the new procedures have or have not added to Parliament's power.

2 Parliamentary Arenas for the Control of Public Spending

By the end of the 1960s Members of Parliament had become aware that while the Executive was developing new methods of control over public spending Parliament retained nineteenth-century procedures ill-suited to scrutinise them. As public spending grew during the 1950s and 1960s, more and more of it entered the category of 'relatively uncontrollable'—much spending was by now in the form of long-term commitments and much of the money was being spent by agencies outside the traditional Central Government departments. Parliamentary opportunities for debating spending plans were still linked to consideration of the annual Departmental Estimates in the traditional procedure of the twenty-nine Supply days and in the Select Committee on Estimates set up in 1912. Yet the Annual Estimates of the Departments by 1968 accounted for only two-thirds of public spending. The recognition of this state of affairs led some Members in the early 1960s to demand alterations in procedure which would allow them opportunities to debate and consider in detail *all* public spending.

At the 1964 election Harold Wilson had promised in a speech at Stowmarket that there would be reform of procedure in the coming Parliament. In the session 1964–65 the Select Committee on Procedure recommended that there should be a system of specialist Select Committees based on consideration of the Estimates. This recommendation closely followed the evidence given to the Committee by the Study of Parliament Group which also suggested that White Papers on Public Expenditure should be presented annually to Parliament and examined by a Select Committee on Expenditure. The Government did not accept the Procedure Committee's recommendations for a system of committees based on consideration of expenditure. It was somewhat nervous about the future role and powers of such committees fearing that they might want to ape the Congressional Committees in the United States of America. Many Members of Parliament preferred the idea of 'subject' specialist committees with wide terms of reference rather than committees set up specifically to scrutinise expenditure. The Government finally produced a compromise solution. New Select Committees were introduced by the Leader of the House, Richard Crossman, in 1966 in the form of 'subject' committees, the first two being Agriculture, and Science and Technology. They were to be an 'experiment' of a limited duration, and were not intended to be the start of a committee system covering the whole range of Governmental activities as had been suggested by the Committee on Procedure.

The Procedure Committee did not give up its interest in the possibility of enhancing Parliament's ability to control the executive through an expenditure-based Select Committee system. It approached the problem of Select Committees from a different angle when in the session 1968–69 it conducted an enquiry into *Scrutiny of Public Expenditure and Administration*.[1] This was a broad survey of the ability of Parliament to control public spending through existing procedures especially in the light of new developments in the Treasury and Departments which had no counterparts in Parliament. The results of this detailed enquiry published in 1969 (35 witnesses gave oral evidence) led the Committee to recommend, firstly, that White Papers on Public Expenditure be presented to Parliament each year and be debated for two days, and secondly, that an Expenditure Committee be set up to allow for the development of new links in the 'circle of control' over public spending. The new procedures would then allow Parliament to discuss long-term expenditure plans, to examine the means being adopted to execute policies, and to make retrospective scrutiny of the results achieved and the value for money obtained. The Committee considered that 'Government decisions, both about the level of public expenditure as a whole, and about the way in which the total amount of public expenditure is allocated between its various components, are among the most important which Ministers take. It is desirable that decisions of such importance should be taken, so far as possible, in the light of public discussion of the issues involved, and that the grounds on which they are taken should be made known to the public.'[2] The White Paper debates would provide an opportunity for public discussion of these decisions, and the grounds on which they had been

---

[1] H.C. 410, Session 1968–69.
[2] *Scrutiny of Public Expenditure and Administration*, H.C. 410 of 1968–69, pp. v–vii.

taken would be subject to scrutiny by the proposed Expenditure Committee.

The Government was, once again, cautious in its response to the Committee's recommendations. It accepted the recommendation that there should be annual Expenditure White Papers presented to Parliament for debate. But it was not particularly keen on the idea of an Expenditure Committee. The Leader of the house, Mr Fred Peart, was engaged in his own feasibility study of the proposal when the 1970 general election intervened and brought the Conservatives to power. The Conservatives were committed to introduce 'A new style of Government' which among other things matched changes in Parliamentary procedure with changes that had taken place in Government machinery. In October 1970 a Green Paper was published setting out the Government's plan for an Expenditure Committee.[3] After a debate on the paper in the House of Commons on 12 November 1970 the new Committee was set up and started work early in 1971.

From October 1970 the new pattern of procedure was established. Both of the recommendations of the Procedure Committee had finally been implemented. On the floor of the House the new procedure for debating the Expenditure White Papers made little difference except for providing a few extra days for debate. Members still retained the existing opportunities to debate public spending whenever new legislation was before the House, on the twenty-nine Supply days, and on adjournment and private members' motions. The new debating procedure was simply piled on top of the older ones. No attempt was made towards a radical reform of the debating procedures. Furthermore, the uses which members made of their debating opportunities in the 1970s reflected the procedural continuity.

The new White Paper debates have since 1970 provided the main opportunity for Members to discuss over-all levels of spending. Although the Government agreed, when instituting the new procedure, to make debating time available, it has in practice rarely been able to provide more than one day's debate per session. When the Opposition has felt that this is insufficient to allow full consideration of the Government's forward spending plans, it has generally been able to extend the debate to two days by using a Supply day in addition to the day made available from Government time. Even so, two days of debate do not allow many Members to take part.

This shortage of time has rarely been deplored by M.P.s for the

[3] *Select Committees of the House of Commons*, Cmnd 4507, October 1970.

reason that few of them have been enthused by the prospect of making a speech on the general issue of public spending. There are many reasons for the general lack of interest in the White Paper debates. The White Papers are based on the annual Public Expenditure Survey (PESC) exercise in which the Government lays down the projections for public spending over the forthcoming five years. PESC surveys have been carried out since the recommendations of the Plowden Committee in 1961, and White Papers based on PESC have been debated in most sessions since 1970. Unfortunately Governments have not been able to produce their White Papers on a regular annual basis. Elections, financial crises, and pressure for changes in previously agreed spending plans have held up publication in most years so that the November publication date has rarely been adhered to. The White Paper due in November 1975, for example, did not appear until March 1976. Publication of and debate on the 1976 White Paper was then delayed as a result of the continued sterling crisis, the failure to control inflation, and the overcrowded Parliamentary schedule. During the period between the publication of the 1975 and 1976 White Papers alterations were made to the 1975 White Paper. When the 1976 White Paper appeared in February 1977, it was found to contain projections merely for two years ahead instead of the customary five. The irregularity with which White Papers have been produced has not ensured for them a secure place in the Parliamentary year like that occupied by the Budget and the Finance Bill.

Another weakness of the new procedure stems from the nature of the White Paper itself. The figures presented in the White Paper do not give Members much concrete evidence of actual levels of public spending in future years, since they are merely projections. Many factors have combined, since the PESC system was inaugurated, to ensure that the figures presented in any one year bear little relation to the actual outturn of money expended. Each successive White Paper has promised one particular level of spending in the forthcoming years and in the event the level has always been different and higher. Since Members can never be sure that a White Paper means what it says, they have little faith in the value of debating something over which they have even less control than the Government.

Members are generally much more interested in spending on individual functions of Government than on the total levels of spending. Until 1976 few were worried about the total level of spending. They were much more concerned with the provision of money for individual and local projects. But the White Paper does not encourage informed debate even on the spending for separate functions of Government. In spite of improvements in presentation in recent years the White Paper does not tell Members much about the policies behind the figures given for spending on the various Governmental functions. Unless a Member is already an expert in a policy area, he cannot tell whether the projected expenditure in that function is too high, too low, or just about right. No 'costed options' are presented for individual functions and there is no information about the overlap of functions and relative importance of one function to another. The assiduous Member who really wants to know what lies behind the figures in the White paper has to consult the work of independent bodies which have recently begun to analyse the Expenditure White Papers.[4] Partly for the reasons above Members of the House of Commons were not encouraged, at least until 1976, to make much use of their opportunity to debate the total level of spending or allocation between the competing functions. In the early years of White Paper debates these were poorly attended and speeches were of a low standard. But by 1976 the question of the total level of public spending in relation to the national output of goods and services had become one of the most significant political questions of the day. The debate on the 1975 Expenditure White Paper (which took place in March 1976) exhibited a new sense of interest and urgency. The issue confronting Members in this debate is neatly summed up in the opening words of the Expenditure White Paper before the House:

> In the past three years public expenditure has grown by nearly 20 per cent in volume while output has risen by less than 2 per cent. The tax burden has greatly increased. The increase in the tax burden has fallen heavily on low wage earners. Those earning less than the average contribute over one quarter of the income tax yield.[5]

Although attendance at the debate was not particularly high, the quality of the speeches was of a different order from the lack lustre speeches of earlier White Paper debates. The 1976 debate contained many references to the need to think carefully and rationally when planning and monitoring public expenditure. There was a recognition

---

[4] The fullest analyses (but of social policy only) are provided by the Centre for Studies in Social Policy. Its publications include: Rudolf Klein (ed.), *Social Policy and Public Expenditure 1974*, and Rudolf Klein (ed.), *Social Policy and Public Expenditure 1975: Inflation and Priorities*.

[5] *Public Expenditure to 1979–80*, Cmnd 6393.

that the Government's (and the taxpayer's) pocket is not bottom-less. Edmund Dell, summing up for the Government, said, 'We have come to the point where we cannot persuade people of the need to pay 50p out of every additional pound that they earn, or perhaps even-tually more.'[6] Members were forced in this debate to think, as never before, about priorities and allocations between functions. They had to concentrate their minds on the fact that higher spending on one function might mean lower spending on another. Mr Dell said of the debate, 'It has been a very fine debate. One might say that it has been the only real debate we have yet had on a Public Expendi-ture White Paper.'[7]

The debate on the White Paper in February 1977 was of even greater interest than that of 1976 because its dramatic result nearly caused the downfall of the Government. In the vote at the end the Government was defeated and saved its existence only by a subsequent vote of confidence and a 'pact' with the Liberals. But the actual vote on the White Paper itself did not technically amount to rejection of the proposals for spending; the Government, sensing trouble, had not allowed the debate to take place on a motion to 'take note' of the paper. Instead, it permitted the debate only on a motion to adjourn the House. Expecting a defeat, the Government reasoned that the loss of such a motion would not be so serious as the loss of a motion to 'take note', which might imply a rejection of the Government's whole programme and therefore threaten its existence.

Even though the 1975 and 1976 (debated 1976 and 1977 respectively) White Papers have caused a little political excitement, the substance of the debates themselves still leaves much to be desired. It is difficult for Members to get fully to grips with the question of desirable levels of total public spending when there is no Parliamentary procedure to allow them to debate spending and taxation together. As Mr Tony Newton said during the 1976 White Paper debate, 'It is clear that we can judge the White Paper properly only when we have the Budget figures.'[8] But in Budget debates there is little mention of expenditure. Members do not seem at all aware of the White Papers on Expenditure when they debate the Budget. This is not surprising when one examines the contents of the Budget statement from the Chancellor which forms the basis for the Budget debate. The Budget statement is largely about taxation. It concerns itself with the management of

[6] H.C. Debates, 10 March 1976, col. 550.
[7] H.C. Debates, 10 March 1976, col. 547.
[8] H.C. Debates, 10 March 1976, col. 506.

the economy, for taxation is used for this purpose, but it rarely says much about the relationship between income and expenditure, between taxation and Government spending. Taxation proposals are presented in some detail. In recent years, especially since 1964, the Budget proposals and consequent Finance Bills have been of ever increasing technical complexity. Members have devoted much of their time in Budget debates to spotting the possible loopholes in proposed new taxes or adjustments to existing taxes, and a considerable amount of time has been taken up even in these debates in pressing local and constituency interests upon the Government. The result of presenting M.P.s with information on spending and taxation at different times is that the integrated information which Members would need for a full and fruitful debate on the total level of public spending is never presented to them. There is no opportunity for a rational discussion of the relationship between expected future income and proposed expenditure. Some M.P.s are beginning to be critical of this defect in procedure. Mr Michael English, Chairman of the General Sub-Committee of the Expenditure Committee, has said, 'Britain is unique ... in considering expenditure separately from taxation.'[9]

Rather than pressing for new procedures which would make Parliamentary consideration of public spending more rational, most Members have continued to focus their attention on the traditional methods of discussing expenditure. They are still able to debate the total of expenditure on individual policies and services and the balance within services during the twenty-nine Supply days each session (on which the subject for debate is selected by the Opposition), on adjournment debates each evening and at the end of the session, on Private Members' motions, and during the Legislative process. They may also use Question time to ask Ministers about levels of public spending in the Departments for which they are responsible, and to ask the Treasury Ministers general questions about levels and control of public spending.

Although the Supply debates are, in theory, about the Government's spending estimates for the coming year, in practice they can be about almost anything. There is no clear connection between the use of these debates and public spending. These twenty-nine days are still called 'Supply' days even though most of the debates concerned take place on motions unconnected with the estimates. The motions are devised by the Opposition to allow it to criticise the Government. In the session 1976–76, for example, one Supply day debate took place on a

9 H.C. Debates, 10 March 1976, col. 512.

motion to reduce the salary of the Secretary of State for Industry by
£1000. This permitted discussion of the motor industry and specifically of the Government's financial support for Chrysler. Much was
said by Members in the debate about the level of financial support
for ailing industries. By chance the motion proposed by the
Opposition was carried and the Government had, the following week,
to introduce another motion to reinstate the salary of the Minister
concerned. This example shows that, even if the Opposition does win
a vote on a Supply day, it is not really exerting the traditional 'power
of the purse', since that vote need not be on an actual estimate. No
Government will consider the loss of such a vote as a call for its
resignation. Supply debates no longer perform the function of control
of public expenditure. In any case the annual estimates of the Government departments do not cover all the annual expenditure of Government. The estimates themselves only cover about 50 per cent of all
public spending—they exclude local authority spending and spending
by the nationalised industries.

During the Supply days the House of Commons still in theory
considers the annual estimates of the Central Government departments,
and could in an adverse vote reject a Government estimate provided
that a suitable motion was brought before it by the Opposition. In
no recent times, however, has the British House of Commons rejected
an estimate.[10]

While retaining apparent and theoretical powers of control through
the Supply procedure, the British House of Commons has today no
real powers over the details of Government spending because it has not
the political will to exercise these powers.[11] Only in the most grave
circumstances where a Government had lost its majority or lost the
confidence of a sufficient number of its supporters would the sanctions
of the Supply process be likely to be invoked. Nor has the British
House of Commons, unlike some other legislatures, any power to alter
the details of indvidual estimates brought before it. The estimates
are voted through or blocked as they are. A motion to reduce an
estimate (the House of Commons has no power to lay a motion to
increase an estimate) is always interpreted by the Government as a
motion to reject it altogether. So Members cannot, as can Members
of the U.S. Congress, influence the Government's spending plans by

[10] Examples of cases where an estimate has been refused are given in Gordon Reid,
The Politics of Financial Control, Hutchinson, London, 1966, and in Andrew Hill and
Anthony Whichelow, *What's Wrong with Parliament*, Penguin, London, 1964.
[11] Unlike the Canadian House of Commons which in 1974 did reject a number of
estimates, thus causing Mr Trudeau to call a general election.

chopping off some sections or adding on others. In Britain the details of spending plans are determined by the Government alone. In the absence of either chance of rejection or powers of detailed alteration all that the British House of Commons can do in the Supply process is to provide a political background against which the Government makes its spending decisions. The Supply days remain the main opportunity for M.P.s to debate matters of Expenditure in the Whole House. For this reason it is worth examining the contents of the Supply debates in some detail so as to discover just what kind of messages Members are sending to the Government about spending when they decide to speak in these debates.

A wide range of topics is selected by the Opposition for debate on its Supply days. Some of these have an obvious connection with spending and invite Members to debate in terms of spending on a particular Governmental function. When however, as in the 1975–76 session, the timetable of Parliament becomes clogged up with an excess of Government legislation, Supply days may be used to debate general policy or urgent matters for which the Government is unwilling to give time. In the 1975–76 session, for example, Supply debates were held on foreign affairs (East-West relations, the European Community (development), and Northern Ireland security. None of these subjects had any noticeable connection with public spending and Members did not refer to expenditure in the debates. In some other debates not obviously connected with expenditure M.P.s nevertheless do take the opportunity to raise the question of spending. In the session 1975–76 during a debate on the fishing industry mainly concerned with the 'Cod War' several Members suggested that subsidies should be paid to the fishing industry. And the debate on personal taxation in the same session turned out to be on the relationship between taxation and public expenditure.

Housing, education, health and other aspects of social policy are among the Supply day topics that have invoked much discussion on expenditure. A study of the contents of such debates shows that, when subjects on which expenditure is considerable are discussed, Members use the opportunity to press demands for higher spending on those functions of Government.[12] Supply debates are used by Members to reflect concerns among the public at large. They convey to the Government what kinds of expenditure Members think that the people

---

[12] The author has made a study of the contents of all Supply debates from the session 1967–68 to 1972–73 and of the session 1975–76. The subjects were classified and an analysis made of the contents.

want, and how much they are prepared to pay for. Because Supply debates are used in this way they perform the function of a 'political pressure gauge', and their contents tell us much about the attitudes of Members and of the public towards public spending.

The general impression gained from reading Supply debates of the 1960s is that M.P.s then used this procedure to press claims upon the Government for higher spending on individual projects and local causes. The claims were related to particular political events and circumstances or to constituency interests. In periods of high unemployment, for example, the number of Supply debates on the subject rose and these contained many requests for higher spending on the support of industry, especially in depressed areas. The debates allowed Members to display to their constituents that they were taking care of their interests and pressing their demands. Debates on housing, education, or health were in the 1960s full of requests for increased spending on the total function or on individual local projects. The one exception to this pattern came in the debates on defence, in which a group of left-wing Labour M.P.s committed to cuts in defence spending demanded reductions. One argument used by this group was that more could be spent on social services if defence spending were cut. Other M.P.s rarely raised arguments of allocation of scarce resources among competing functions—they simply claimed more resources for their causes. On the whole, Supply debates in the 1960s provided a platform for the presentation of uncoordinated and unrelated demands for higher spending. The uncoordinated nature of these debates was heightened by the way in which Members failed to sit through entire debates listening to all points of view but simply made their entrance, stated their case, and left the chamber as soon as decently possible after their speeches. The chamber was rarely full for Supply debates, which became a series of statements and requests rather than real interchanges of ideas.

By the mid-1970s the pattern of opinions about public spending reaching the Government from the House of Commons had begun to change from the free-spending attitudes of the 1960s. Members were being pressured in a new way by constituents who were concerned at the level of income tax which by 1976 was being levied on workers earning far less than the average wage. This together with the constant problem of the Government's never declining borrowing requirement had its effect on M.P.s' attitudes towards public expenditure. Many began to notice that more spent on one function would have to mean less spent on another. They discovered that public expenditure could only grow above the 1976 levels if the economy also grew, for there was a limit to taxing and borrowing. A further reason for the change in attitude in the mid-1970s, as revealed in Supply debates, was that a Conservative party formed the major portion of the Opposition. In spite of its own past record as a generous spender, it was by the mid-1970s firmly committed to control of, and reductions in, the level of public expenditure. It was supported in this view by the Liberal party.

Members still called for increased spending on some items, but most were more restrained than in earlier periods. There is one exception to this pattern. Just as, in the mid-1960s, a group of left-wing Labour M.P.s stood against the trend by calling for cuts in defence spending, so in the 1970s a number of Conservatives generally opposed to increased expenditure stoutly argue that cuts in defence spending have gone too far and that spending on defence should actually be increased. In the 1960s Members talked and thought about expenditure in terms of requests for higher spending on individual items. Increased spending by Government was bolstered up by a free-spending attitude from the House of Commons. The Government in the mid-1970s found a different background to its decisions. Members of the Opposition parties were not the only ones now demanding that public spending be kept under control and that Governments should keep to their announced plans—although they were the loudest calling for actual cuts. The Government, slow to respond at first (perhaps for political reasons), had by 1976 adopted the Opposition view of public expenditure and instituted a system of 'cash limits', as well as stringent controls on the total expenditure.

The same basic patterns of opinion have been found in the uses made of other opportunities for debate in the Whole House. Debates on the adjournment and on Private Members' motions have been used sometimes to comment upon 'general policy' but more often to make claims for higher spending on individual and local items such as housing and hospital building. In periods of high unemployment they have been used to vent grievances from particularly hard-hit regions or constituencies. The demands reaching the Government from such debates have however been fragmented and uncoordinated. Members speaking have not related their specific demands to total levels of spending, nor have they often recognised that the particular demands may only be fulfilled at the expense of some other item. The short duration of these debates has allowed time only for one or two speeches and so there has been little consideration of the relative merits or demerits of the case from a number of angles.

Finally, the passage of new legislation has provided Members with an opportunity to consider public spending. New legislation brought before the House must, if it imposes a charge upon the taxpayer, be accompanied by Financial Resolutions which have to be considered by the Whole House. Debates on these Resolutions, however, add little to the ability of the House to control public spending because no attempt is made during the course of them to link new proposals for spending to the total existing levels or to the amount of spending already committed to other related items. There may be some discussion of the general costs involved in a new Bill, but, as the example of the ill-fated Devolution Bill of 1977 shows, the Government itself may have little concrete and precise information as to the actual long-term costs consequent upon the legislation. Moreover, each item of legislation is considered separately, so that the general effect of legislation debates is like the general effect of other debates: they provide the Government merely with fragmented and uncoordinated opinion. The weakness of Parliamentary control through the legislative process has recently been criticised in the following manner:

> The public expenditure decisions that will flow from the Act and which will be reflected in the Annual Estimates of future years cannot be separated from the decision on the bill itself ... perhaps the interrelationship between policy and legislative decision on the one hand and expenditure planning and allocation on the other needs to be reconsidered in the House of Commons.[13]

Adjournment, Private Members' and Legislative debates fulfil the function of a political pressure gauge as Supply debates do. They provide the Government with some indication of the general sentiments of the House with respect to the strength of support for particular items of expenditure. The pressure gauge is not, however, a completely accurate mechanism for the conveyance of opinion, and the Government must be aware of this. Debates are to some extent a distorting mirror of opinion reflecting as much the intensity of feelings about public spending as the extent of demands for particular functions of Government. If all the debates containing references to expenditure are added together, it is found that in most sessions since 1967 the most popular subject in terms of time allowed for debate has been Defence. Yet Defence is by no means the largest single item in the Government's total spending. It is an item on which intense feelings

---

[13] Michael Ryle, 'The Commons in the Seventies—a General Survey', in S. A. Walkland and Michael Ryle (eds), *The Commons in the Seventies*, p. 30.

for and against are felt among a small proportion of Members. So strong has the interest been that, although Defence debates have been generally sparsely attended and dominated by a small group of M.P.s, there has been no reduction in the amount of time made available for the subject. Second to Defence in terms of debating time comes Employment and Industry—an item on which relatively little is spent. It is popular because unemployment is an emotive issue and thought to be cured by greater expenditure on the creation of new jobs. Quite a long way behind these two items in the popularity stakes come the largest spending subjects of Housing, Education and Health. All other functions get only a small proportion of the total debating time.

To what extent is the Government influenced by the debates in the House of Commons? Do debates on levels and allocations of public spending have any impact on the Government at all or do they simply confirm it in its own views? During the 1960s and early 1970s the Government was supported in its expansion of public spending by the effects of the nature of debate in the House. Some pressures for increased spending still persist in the retrenching days of the late 1970s, but it must be said that certain M.P.s are now in the position of being able to say to the Government: 'I told you so', in so far as they have for a considerable time been pressing the Government to check the expansion of expenditure. However there might also be a case for saying that, rather than being influenced by the change of direction in Parliamentary debates, the Government was finally forced by economic circumstances and the influence of the IMF to check expenditure growth. This change of direction of policy was not popular among some of the Government's supporters. While the Government may have known as well as the Opposition what steps it had to take, it held its hand for several months for fear of an unpleasant confrontation in Parliament from a section of its party. Finally events took such a course that the confrontation issue became an irrelevance; retrenchment had to be instituted regardless. The IMF loan settlement of November 1976 imposed conditions of restriction on Government spending and borrowing. These events illustrate how severely limited the power of the British Parliament is over the spending of the Government. It may delay certain actions for a while but cannot stop them. If for the pressing needs of the economy or for stabilising the balance of payments the Government is forced to take particular measures, it will, rather than bow to Parliamentary opinion, take the chance that in the last analysis Members of Parliament, fearing for their own personal and party futures, will go along with what the Government decides.

If debate on the floor of the House is an uncertain route to Parliamentary control over public spending, what alternative procedures are available to the individual Member wishing to influence Government decisions? It is sometimes suggested that one of the more powerful weapons in the hands of the House is the practice of Question Time, when Ministers are held answerable for their actions and for the actions of their Departments. Members can use Question Time to probe the Government's spending and employ this procedure to obtain information on specific expenditure items as well as on the general issue. Question Time is often used for the same purpose as debates—to point out shortcomings in spending on particular items. The Member will put down a question asking for information about spending on an item or about provision of a particular service, and then come in with a supplementary and comments deprecating the fact that Government spends so little on that service. Questions may also be asked of the Treasury Ministers about general facets of public expenditure—on, for example, the size of the Public Sector Borrowing Requirement or on rates and incidence of taxation. These questions may be tabled by those who wish to deplore the over-all spending levels. The disadvantage of the Question Time procedure, so far as the ordinary Member is concerned, is that the amount of information obtainable through questions is limited by the shortness of the question hour and the rota system which ensures that individual Ministers face the Commons infrequently.[14] Moreover the procedure does not really provide any true sanctions on a Minister with respect to public spending, for there have been no cases of Ministers resigning through ill-conceived or ill-carried out spending plans. Short of cases of criminal negligence it is difficult to see how blame could be attached to a Minister with respect to spending decisions when so many of these are a collective Cabinet responsibility.

One of the best methods of obtaining information about public spending available to the Member is to join one of the Select Committees that have a function of financial oversight. A popular Committee with M.P.s is the Public Accounts Committee set up by Gladstone in 1861 to complete the 'circle of control' by which Parliament first authorised expenditure through the Supply process

---

[14] For a full discussion of the limits of Question Time in general see Sir Norman Chester, 'Questions in the House', in S. A. Walkland and Michael Ryle (eds), *The Commons in the Seventies*, pp. 149–174.

and later checked on the actual spending to see that it had been carried out as Parliament intended. The Public Accounts Committee (PAC) receives from the office of the Comptroller and Auditor General the accounts of Government departments and of some other bodies that spend public funds such as the universities. These accounts have been examined in detail by the 600 or so staff of the Comptroller's office to see that the money was actually spent in accordance with the details set out in the Annual Estimates. The PAC picks out from the mass of documents a number of subjects for its own detailed investigation and comment.

The power of the PAC is commonly held to reside in its ability to call before it civil servants to account for their actions. Fear of having to appear before the Committee is supposed to keep civil servants on their toes. But in any one session a Committee of some fifteen M.P.s can only interview a small number of civil servants, so that the probability of any individual civil servant having to account for errors in this way is low. Even if peculiar dealings were to go on each year in Government departments, universities and other bodies, the PAC would not have the time to look at them all. Another problem for the Committee is how to draw the line between correct and incorrect actions. In the past fifteen years civil servants have lived in an atmosphere where overspending is the rule rather than the exception, and where the scope of spending is so large that some errors of judgement are bound to occur. Once a project has started little can be done to stop it regardless of its inefficiency. The Swansea Licensing Bureau has become a symbol of the way Government departments and agencies may overspend without fear of punishment. The PAC may have complained that the delays, lack of preparatory work, and the inexperience of those concerned meant that this Bureau cost £13.5m more than was intended and that running costs remain higher than estimated with staff 50 per cent higher than forecast.[15] But a rap on the knuckles from the PAC has not put the clock back. The Swansea Licensing Bureau continues on its costly way.

The Chairman of the PAC in 1977 has himself expressed considerable concern about the inability of Parliament to control spending or to influence Government plans. In a pamphlet entitled *Parliament and the Purse Strings* published in May 1977 he outlined many weaknesses in both the Government's and Parliament's methods of controlling spending. The Government for its part is weak at forecasting and checking expenditure so that 'Outturn rarely accords with forecast

[15] *Fourth Report of the Public Accounts Committee, 1974–5*, H.C. 502.

and government expenditure is still very much out of control.'[16] Parliament no longer plays its proper part in ensuring that Governments do control their spending. 'Instead of divisive arguments over whether or not there should be cuts in expenditure the House would be a more admired place if members united to enforce a control.'[17] In the first place, Mr du Cann suggests, Parliament should pay more attention to the annual debate on the Expenditure White Paper so that this would become the most significant of all Parliament's regular debates. Secondly the present arrangements for detailed scrutiny in Select Committees are ineffective. Both the Public Accounts Committee and the Expenditure Committee are, in Mr du Cann's view, 'scrambling about on the tip of an expenditure iceberg' and there is no Select Committee to consider taxation. He recommends that the Select Committee system should be reformed to produce a scrutiny or monitoring committee that would absorb the functions of the PAC, the Expenditure Committee and the Nationalised Industries Committee. This new committee should have a number of sub-committees to include one concerned with taxation. The present staffing arrangements of Select Committees would be altered by giving the proposed new Committee access to the staff of the Comptroller and Auditor General's office.

It is significant that as late as 1977 there are still further proposals for strengthening Parliamentary control over spending through the establishment of yet more new Select Committees. This brings us back to the two new procedures introduced in 1970 including the establishment of the Expenditure Committee. This chapter has already shown how the White Paper debates have failed to enhance Parliament's control. The whole point of the Expenditure Committee was that it too should improve Parliamentary ability to influence patterns of public spending. Yet the implications of the PAC Chairman's suggestion are not only that his committee is inadequate but that the new Expenditure Committee has not lived up to expectations. The final paragraph of the Procedure Committee report of 1968–69, in which the establishment of the Expenditure Committee was urged reads:

The extent of control by the House of Commons of public expenditure depends on the relationship between the House and the Executive. Although there are limits to the degree to which governments can be expected to disclose their plans and future thinking,

[16] Edward du Cann, *Parliament and the Purse Strings: How to bring Public Expenditure under Parliamentary Control*, Conservative Political Centre, London, 1977, p. 5.

[17] *Ibid*, p. 7.

yet over the years the power of the executive has tended to increase, and this tendency has left its mark on the working of Parliament. Your Committee believe that the main outline of the proposed changes in procedure should be embarked upon without delay if the House is to develop its proper influence in those fields.[18]

But what did the Procedure Committee think that 'relationship between the House and the Executive' ought to be? What were the expectations of the role of the new Committee? While all members of the Committee were unanimous in their acceptance of the report, not all of them saw their proposals in precisely the same light. Some thought that the new Expenditure Committee would simply restore some of the detailed scrutiny and check over Government administration which had inevitably been lost in the manner in which Supply procedures had been used by Members over the past seventy years. Some, however, went further and expected that the new Expenditure Committee would enable Members to exert a greater direct influence over the Executive's decisions regarding public expenditure. The different expectations of the role of the Expenditure Committee must now be explored.

[18] H.C. 410 of 1968–69, p. xviii.

3 Expectations of the Role of the Expenditure Committee

> Most of the proposals for alleviating the decay of the House of Commons are met with the rejoinder: 'will it work?' By this what is usually meant is: 'will it work without in any way altering the present dominance of the Executive?' Reports by Select Committees on Procedure or by academic pamphleteers are pointless until the primary question is decided. How much power should the Executive have and how far is it desirable that either the public or a representative chamber should know about or participate in the processes of government?
>
> John P. Mackintosh, *The British Cabinet*,
> Stevens, London, 1962, p. 525.

Six years after John Mackintosh had reminded readers of *The British Cabinet* that a primary question of the balance of power between Executive and Legislature had to be answered before procedural changes were proposed, he himself was a member of the Select Committee on Procedure which recommended the establishment of the Expenditure Committee. Had the Procedure Committee answered the primary question? In the last paragraph of their report[1] they had posed it, but analysis of what the members of that Committee thought the Expenditure Committee was going to do reveals that they had very different views of the proper relative power of Parliament and the Executive and thus of the proper future role of an Expenditure Committee. Indeed the expressed views not only of the members of the Procedure Committee but also of the witnesses to that Committee, of other Members of Parliament in the debates when the Expenditure Committee was set up, and of academic and other commentators, displayed a great variety of opinion both on the desirable balance of power in the constitution and on the prospects for any procedural changes. One idea, however, that all held in common was that power over public spending was somehow shared between just two elements of the Constitution, the Executive and the Legislature. Few took any cognisance of other factors in the spending process.

The different views of the role of the Expenditure Committee were based first of all on theoretical notions respecting the proper role of

[1] *The Scrutiny of Public Expenditure and Administration*, H.C. 410 of 1968–69, p. xviii.

Parliament in the Constitution and secondly on a certain amount of personal experience of committee work on a variety of different types of legislative committees. Certainly the views of the members of the Procedure Committee and other M.P.s who spoke in debates on the subject in 1969 and 1970 were coloured as much by their personal experiences and their own opinions of the value of Select Committees in the political processes as they were by careful examination of the theoretical views of the Parliamentary role. Expectations of the future role of the Expenditure Committee were not based on any very clear concepts of the roles of Select Committees, for there was little to go on. Such academic studies of Select Committees as had been made prior to 1970 described and listed the works of Select Committees but provided little concrete evidence of the behaviour patterns of committee members.[2]

There were a number of differing views about the proper balance of power between Executive and Legislature behind the expectations of the Expenditure Committee's future. All these views, however, shaded into one another, being ranged along a continuum. At one end of the continuum Parliament was, and is, seen to have relatively little power vis-a-vis the Executive. According to this 'minimalist' view of Parliamentary power the Government governs and Parliament legitimises the Government's acts. This view of Parliament is commonly held by those who support a system of strong party Government and strict party discipline within the Legislature. It tends to be popular among those who take an ideological view of politics. In the 1930 both G. D. H. Cole and Harold Laski thought that the Labour Party, when it came to power, would have to minimise the power of Parliament to ensure that its legislation passed.[3] The two most recent supporters of the minimalist model of Parliament's power are Michael Foot and Enoch Powell, both of whom dislike the idea of Select Committees and consider them nests of consensus politics incompatible with strong party rule.[4]

[2] K. C. Wheare, *Government by Committee*, Clarendon Press, Oxford, 1955, provided useful insights into general patterns of committee work in Government. The other two major works on committees were: David Coombes, *The Member of Parliament and the Administration*, Allen and Unwin, London, 1966, and Nevil Johnson, *Parliament and Administration: The Estimates Committee*, Allen and Unwin, London, 1966. Comments on the Financial Select Committees were also available in Basil Chubb, *The Control of Public Expenditure*, Oxford University Press, 1952.

[3] G. D. H. Cole, *A Plan for Britain*, Clarion Pamphlet, London, 1933; Harold J. Laski, *Democracy in Crisis*, W. H. Allen, London, 1933.

[4] See the evidence of Enoch Powell before the Select Committee on Procedure, and the statements of Michael Foot who was a member of that committee, *Specialist Committees*, H.C. 303, 1964–65.

At the other end of the continuum Parliament is regarded as the supreme body in the British Constitution with a role of controller of the Executive. This 'maximalist' view of the proper role of Parliament has never been as popular in Britain as it is in the United States of America where it is enshrined in the Constitutional provisions for separation of powers and the system of checks and balances. Of all classic British political theorists only Jeremy Bentham has made out a sustained case for a strong Parliament which *directs* the Government. Those taking a maximalist view of Parliamentary powers believe that the House of Commons should undertake detailed investigations of all Governmental activities, that the Government should provide Parliament with the necessary information for these investigations, and that Members should be free to make up their own minds and vote according to rational thought rather than the dictates of their parties. Those accepting this view of the role of Parliament— and perhaps we should include John Mackintosh in this category— like the idea of Select Committees with strong powers of investigation and with the ability to force the Government to take heed of their findings. They hoped that the Expenditure Committee would start the process of tipping the balance of the Constitution towards the Legislature and away from the Executive.

Somewhere in between the extremes of minimalist and maximalist answers to Mackintosh's question come those 'moderates' who believe that the Commons' role as a representative body is to act as lay critic of the Executive—to keep it from straying too far off the path desired by the electorate but not to presume to be an expert counter-executive trying to run the country. This view of Parliament's role is perhaps the most popular of all in Britain and has a long history. J. S. Mill, for example, stated in 1861 (the year in which the Public Accounts Committee was set up, incidentally) that Parliament should not do what it was not fitted to do, namely to govern, but should take means to ensure that governing was well done. He continued:

> Instead of the function of governing, for which it is radically unfit, the proper office of a representative assembly is to watch and control the government; to throw the light of publicity on its acts; to compel a full exposition and justification of all of them which any one considers questionable; to censure them if found condemnable, and, if the men who compose the government abuse their trust, or fulfil it in a manner which conflicts with the deliberate sense of the nation, to expel them from office.[5]

[5] J. S. Mill, *On Representative Government*, Everyman Edn., London, 1948, (first published 1861), p. 239.

The moderate view of the role of Parliament vis-a-vis the Executive has long been popular with academic commentators and theorists from Blackstone to Crick via Bagehot and Jennings. Taken from this standpoint a limited role for Select Committees is permissible; but they must not be allowed to become so powerful that they try to take on Governmental duties for which they are unfitted. Kenneth Wheare in *Government by Committee* discusses the role of Select Committees as scrutinising bodies overseeing the Administration and Executive and checking to see that the Executive is really acting in line with Parliament's intentions. The role of Select Committees, as he sees it, is that of watchdog or 'economy hawk', rather on the model of the Public Accounts Committee. The moderate view of the role of Parliament has also been accepted by Nevil Johnson in *Parliament and Administration* (1966), although it is interesting to note that this author has expressed doubt in more recent writings about the validity of the minimalist role of Parliamentary power for the political conditions of the 1970s.[6] His view, based on his study of the Estimates Committee at work, is that Select Committees are most suited for the kind of detailed work which involves the scrutiny function and which does not generally bring out party strife (assuming that there are ideologically different parties in the House from which the committee members are drawn).

The vagueness of the moderate view of Parliament's role permits a great variety of different interpretations of the precise limits to Parliament's power and a great variety of opinions too on the exact role which the Expenditure Committee ought to play. It also in practice allowed the Members on the Procedure Committee—most of whom were moderates—to reach agreement on the general nature of the Expenditure Committee, agreement which would have been much more difficult or else impossible to obtain had too many taken up extreme minimalist or maximalist positions. Only one Member, John Mackintosh, was thought to hold particularly strong views. One of his colleagues in the Committee said of him: 'He has a special view on

[6] Nevil Johnson, 'Select Committees as Tools of Parliamentary Reform', in S. A. Walkland and Michael Ryle (eds), *The Commons in the Seventies*, pp. 175–201. Johnson distinguishes two models of the Parliamentary role, one of the 'majority' model which sees the Legislature as primarily a place for public debate, for presenting a challenge to a Government, and for sustaining a Government. Here there are coherent parties and majority rule. The other model he calls the 'bargaining' model where there are several parties, or parties internally divided. Under the majority model the Legislature as an institution tends to be weak; under the bargaining model it is somewhat stronger. In Britain, Johnson argues, the majority model is not supported by the present system, but the Government still behaves as though it had a normal majority.

the Constitution; it comes out in his writings'.[7] The chairman of the Committee himself referred to the process of building a consensus view in the Committee:

> We have what I call 'Ancient and Modern' on the Select Committee. We have some of the very newest Hon. Members and some of us who have been here rather too long. This Ancient and Modern approach brings out rather good hymns provided that we blend the hymn as we go along.[8]

David Watt (who was acquainted with a number of the Procedure Committee members) writing in *The Financial Times*, thought that the various streams of thought that went into the production of the report had led to 'a fairly classic confusion of aims'.

> The radicals have managed to import the phrase about 'reporting on progress made by Departments towards clarifying their general objectives and priorities' because they feel that this will give MPs the key to discussing any policy decision they choose. The Conservatives, in the next paragraph, have made it clear that they still propose to leave 'policy making' to Ministers; and the modernists have gone haring after the need to introduce up-to-date management methods, 'programme budgeting', 'accountable management' and so on—to Whitehall. Between them all, the Government and the Civil Service seem quite likely to slip through the net altogether.[9]

The Labour Government in 1969, however, had a clear minimalist view and feared that a new Expenditure Committee might prove the thin end of the wedge leading to a shift in the balance of the constitution. Giving evidence to the Procedure Committee, John Diamond, then Chief Secretary to the Treasury, said:

> The appropriate place for challenging policy must be on the Floor of the House on Supply days. The appropriate place for challenging the execution of a policy decision is best carried out (sic) by the Estimates Committee or the Public Accounts Committee where expert evidence is brought forward but where the policy cannot be challenged. And this is the dividing line.[10]

However the Government were careful not to express their fears about the proposed new Committee too clearly in public and instead made

[7] Interview quoted in A. Robinson, 'Select Committees and the Function of Parliament', Unpublished Ph.D. dissertation, McGill University, 1972, p. 192.

[8] H.C. Debates, 21 October 1969, col. 975.

[9] David Watt, *The Financial Times*, 24 October 1969.

[10] Report of the Select Committee on Procedure, *Scrutiny of Public Expenditure and Administration*, H.C. 410 of 1968–69, p. 166, para 552.

general statements as to the momentous nature of the proposal. In the debate held on the Procedure Committee report on 21 October 1969, the Leader of the House, Fred Peart, said: 'A Select Committee on Expenditure would perform the function of strengthening the control of the House over public expenditure and so strengthen the position of the House vis-à-vis the Executive.'[11] In his view the proposal for the Expenditure Committee represented 'a coherent and radical approach to one of the most fundamental problems facing us, namely the balance of power and influence between the House and the Executive'.[12]

Other M.P.s of the minimalist school expressed reservations about the proposed Committee during the same debate. John Mendleson feared that the Expenditure Committee would become a policy-making body, and contemporaneously strike at the root of the strong party system:

> Let there be more efficiency but let everyone realise that the only effective control of the Executive lies in an increase in the number of independent minded Hon. Members who are devoted to the principles and philosophy of their party.[13]

Eric Heffer—who believed that policy was made essentially in the Cabinet and to a lesser extent in Departments, in party meetings, and in the Chamber of the House—also expressed anxiety that the Expenditure Committee might try to make policy:

> When I have listened to a number of Hon. Members I get the impression that once we have established the Sub-committees they will determine policy. That is not true. It is a figment of the imagination to think that. That is called Participation ... I do not know what 'Participation' means. If it means participation in the sense of discussing something that has already been decided and trying to influence it slightly in another direction, that is all right. But it must be understood that that is the limit and we cannot go further in that direction.[14]

Committees, he suggested, could do no more than 'influence' policy. In the debates held on the Procedure Committee's report on 21 October 1969 and on the Conservative Government's Green Paper on Select Committees on 12 November 1970 moderate opinion was

[11] H.C. Debates, 21 October 1969, col. 967.
[12] H.C. Debates, 21 October 1969, col. 970.
[13] H.C. Debates, 21 October 1969, col. 1031.
[14] H.C. Debates, 21 October 1969, col, 1056.

uppermost. This moderate view was of several shades, from the limited to the progressivist. Among the more conservative in outlook was Selwyn Lloyd, a Member of the 1968–69 Procedure Committee. He was careful to draw a distinction between a Committee which scrutinised the Executive and one which controlled it. The new Expenditure Committee would, he thought, 'improve the House's ability to scrutinise public expenditure; not to control it'.[15] He expressed a similar opinion in an article in *The Observer* shortly after the Procedure Committee had reported:

> I really believe that the acceptance of our proposals would be a notable step forward in Parliament recovering the power effectively to scrutinise the performance of the executive. And that ought to be one of Parliament's most important jobs.[16]

Austin Albu and Robin Turton, also members of the Procedure Committee, put forward variants of the limited role of scrutiny of the Executive. Austen Albu, a former accountant, considered that the proper role for the new Committee would be 'an examination of the methods by which decisions are arrived at and the control of effectiveness'.[17] Robin Turton quoted the evidence to the Procedure Committee from the Study of Parliament Group (itself committed at this period to a moderate view of Parliamentary power): 'Parliamentary control ... means influence, not direct control; advice, not command; criticism, not obstruction; scrutiny, not initiative; and publicity, not secrecy.'[18] A more precise definition of the limits of the scrutiny role was outlined by John Boyd Carpenter. He thought that the new Committee should not concern itself with setting political objectives but: 'It will be on firm ground when, accepting the objective, it investigates whether that objective is being achieved economically and efficiently or whether money is being wasted in its pursuit.'[19]

Some M.P.s expected that the Committee would perform a slightly wider function than that of simple scrutiny of the Executive, though not a function which would give it greater power or detract from the floor of the House. They were particularly keen to see the new Committee provide the House of Commons with more information regarding the work of the Executive. Robert Sheldon, who later became a member of the Expenditure Committee, spoke of the vast

[15] H.C. Debates, 21 October 1969, col. 975.
[16] *The Observer*, 20 October 1969.
[17] H.C. Debates, 21 October 1969, col. 998.
[18] H.C. Debates, 12 November 1970, col. 674.
[19] H.C. Debates, 12 November 1970, col. 634.

amount of information about public spending in the hands of the Government. He suggested that 'the real task therefore, which a Member of Parliament has to perform, is to get that knowledge.'[20] He believed that the Expenditure Committee could help Members to get it. Robert Turton said:

> We (the Procedure Committee) tried to think of ways by which more information could be given to Hon. Members not merely in some Committee but in such a way that they could have adequate debates on public expenditure in the House.[21]

Another former member of the Procedure Committee, David Howell, supported this view of the role of the Expenditure Committee, saying that the value of the new Committee would lie in the information which it would present to the House to allow the Chamber to have more informed debates on the Government's spending plans: 'A select committee on Expenditure, far from having the effect of further weakening the Chamber of the House of Commons, would vastly strengthen and enliven debate in the chamber.'[22]

According to John Mackintosh the information which the Expenditure Committee would extract from the Government would have even wider implications than simply making debates livelier on the floor of the House:

> We are talking about an attempt to build up knowledge and information among members, about attempts to raise the quality of debate, and there is the whole value of the activity of the Committee in pressing the Government by bringing members of the Government, Civil Servants, and outside experts into touch and pressing them to explain their objectives.[23]

The idea that Select Committees' function was to produce a report which would then lead to a debate in the House was out of date, he thought. The purpose of Select Committees should be much broader:

> Their work should consist of unravelling the information, teasing out the policy problems, revealing the options and the direction of the Government, so that the House can take the material and then have a big political clash about the issue.[24]

David Marquand, another of the progressivists on the Procedure

[20] H.C. Debates, 21 October 1969, col. 1038.
[21] H.C. Debates, 12 November 1970, col. 660.
[22] H.C. Debates, 21 January 1970, col. 585.
[23] H.C. Debates, 12 November 1970, col. 684.
[24] H.C. Debates, 12 November 1970, col. 685.

Committee, was somewhat sceptical of the function of information gathering if it did not lead to greater power for the House of Commons:

> The purpose of Select Committees is not so that Hon. Members can take part in an interesting academic seminar about problems of technology, education, and so on. Their purpose is to provide Parliament with some countervailing influence to the tremendous growth in the power of the Executive over the last century.[25]

If Parliament wished to control the Executive, said Mr Marquand, then it must possess the key to the Executive door, the key of financial control. He expressed the hope that the Expenditure Committee would give the House that key.

Another ambition of those few Members whose views lay near the maximalist end of the continuum was that the Expenditure Committee would obtain for the House of Commons a greater share in the decision making process. William Hamilton took the view that:

> The important reason for having a committee is not so much the debate that results in the House from its report, but the influence that it should, and does, have on the Government by making their Civil Servants and, under the proposals in the Green Paper, the Ministers concerned, come to the committees. It puts them on their mettle to justify the policy decisions they are making.[26]

And James Johnson put the case for the Expenditure Committee as a policy making machine in even stronger terms:

> I believe that we should not only attempt to correct excesses, deficits, and wastage in the public purse, but take a share in decision making.... Such committees can force a Government to change some aspects of their policy. In that way, Members of Parliament can share in decision making.... We should not be inhibited from considering policy in its formative stages.[27]

Peter Jay, writing in *The Times*, expected the Expenditure Committee to give the House of Commons a greater share in the decision making process because it would allow the House 'to monitor the activities of the executive at the formative stage: namely when and where the strategic allocations of resources are made'.[28] Later, in evidence to the General sub-committee of the Expenditure Com-

---

[25] H.C. Debates, 21 October 1969, col. 1007.
[26] H.C. Debates, 12 November 1970, col. 693.
[27] H.C. Debates, 12 November 1970, cols. 713, 714, and 716.
[28] *The Times*, 6 November 1969.

mittee when in its first year it was trying to define its own role, Jay stated that its job would be 'to challenge, to probe and perchance to influence'.[29] He was here in fact paraphrasing Patrick Jenkin, who had said that the Expenditure Committee could 'enable Hon. Members to challenge, to probe, and then to influence . . . perhaps the Legislature could begin to regain some control over that huge benign, secretive, remorseless juggernaut that we call administration'.[30]

Those newspapers and journals commenting on the proposal for the Expenditure Committee saw in it hopes for a more powerful Legislature, and for this reason they all welcomed it. However, it should be remembered that some of those writing articles in the Press were members of the Procedure Committee (for example, Selwyn Lloyd in *The Observer*, David Marquand in *New Society*, and David Howell in *The Times*), and others had been associated with the movement towards greater Parliamentary control over public spending (like Peter Jay). Among other, less personally connected, commentators one writer in *The Scotsman* regarded the proposals as 'revolutionary', and added that 'they are a decided step in the right direction and the report could mark a watershed in the history of Parliament';[31] while *The Guardian* suggested that the Expenditure Committee would enable the House of Commons 'to take part effectively in a vital decision making process which Ministers and departments have so far kept to themselves. Parliament could also participate again'.[32]

While there was much optimism in the expectations of what the Expenditure Committee might do, one or two notes of caution were sounded. An effective Expenditure Committee would need staff to help it if it were properly to investigate Government activities and take a part in the shaping of policy. John Boyd Carpenter said that the Expenditure Committee would not be able to work properly without staff like those available to the Public Accounts Committee:

> If the new Committee is to work efficiently, this is not just a question of giving it one or two extra clerks. . . . It involves equipping it with a real investigating staff of its own. We are kidding ourselves if we think that an assembly of very busy Members of this House with, as we know, many other commitments and obligations sitting perhaps twice a week for a couple of hours, can possibly get

[29] Evidence to the Expenditure Committee, 17 May 1970, H.C. 549, 1970–71, p. 93, para 1.
[30] H.C. Debates, 22 January 1970, col. 828.
[31] *The Scotsman*, 20 September 1969.
[32] *The Guardian*, 20 September 1969.

at what is referred to in the Green Paper as ... 'the reasons and policies behind the figures' unless there is a staff. ... How can the ablest of Members of Parliament hope to extract from the representative of a great department of state the facts which such a committee wishes to discover and which perhaps the department does not want to disclose, unless the committee has some of the briefing advantages bestowed so lavishly on the witnesses appearing before it.[33]

Without adequate briefing, he feared, members of the new Committee might soon become disillusioned. John Mackintosh also took the view that the Committee could not hope to become influential if it were not adequately staffed:

The staff of the Committees must be improved beyond all measure. I agree that the staff and specialists should be servants of the House, but it is not sufficient to expect a Clerk of the House, however brilliant, hardworking and assiduous, to cope with two Specialist Committees as well as spend time on other business and the Council of Europe.[34]

But perhaps we can let William Hamilton have the last word on this point: 'I consider that time and the cult of amateurism are the twin enemies of adequate control of the Executive by the Legislature.'[35] Here Hamilton was attacking what Nevil Johnson has described as 'one of the most fundamental beliefs in British social and political life. This is that the best critic is the lay critic ... our society is pervaded by this belief.'[36]

Very few Members of Parliament and few commentators at the time saw the prospects for the Expenditure Committee in any terms save those of Executive/Legislature relations. Few seemed aware of factors other than these two in the policy-making process. Among the twenty or thirty speeches made in the House of Commons on the 1970 proposals to establish the Committee, scarcely any reached beyond the issue of adjusting the balance of power between Executive and Parliament. Only those Members with recent experience of working on the new Crossman committees had any glimmerings of what else the Expenditure Committee, with its wide terms of reference, might do. Arthur Bottomley, who was then chairman of one of the new specialist committees, spoke of an aspect of Select Committee

[33] H.C. Debates, 12 November 1970, col. 632.
[34] H.C. Debates, 21 October 1969, col. 1021.
[35] H.C. Debates, 12 November 1970, col. 697.
[36] Nevil Johnson, *Parliament and Administration: the Estimates Committee, 1945–65*, London, 1966, p. 169.

work which, although it had been recognised in the nineteenth century when Select Committees were commonly used to collect information about topics of national concern, had been largely forgotten in the twentieth.

> My experience as Chairman of the Select Committee on Race Relations and Immigration has taught me that the Committee machinery is a very valuable means of improving contact between Ministers and Civil Servants and groups and individuals in the community. They are an essential method of improving contact between Government departments and Parliament. They provide an opportunity for information and ideas to flow in both directions.... There is also an opportunity provided for people outside Parliament to put their views.[37]

A broader concept of the future role of the Expenditure Committee was also put forward in a paper circulated among academics by an anonymous civil servant. Three 'ideal types' of committee function were identified in the paper. These types were: the lobbyist, the independent critic, and the partner. In the lobbyist model a body interposed between the Executive decision making process and particular interest groups serves to represent client interests while preserving a fair measure of independence from those interests. The author of the paper thought that the five policy-area-based sub-committees of the Expenditure Committee might have some tendency to identify with particular sectional interests. However, it could be that each sub-committee would have such wide spheres of interest that this bias might be mitigated. He personally thought that the most logical and constitutionally appropriate role for the Expenditure Committee was that of an independent lay critic of the Executive like the Public Accounts Committee. But he wondered at the same time whether the Expenditure Committee could in practice perform this scrutinising role. He had three reasons for doubt. If the Expenditure Committee were to stray into areas of policy, party loyalties might come under and cause strain. If the Expenditure Committee was to be independent of the Government, it would need an independent source of and control over information. In the case of expenditure plans much of the information relevant to the Committee's work would have to come from the Government. It was for this last reason that the author thought that the role of partner to the Government was one which the Committee would most likely develop. The Committee would become, not a thorn in the flesh of the Executive, as some Ministers apparently feared, but

[37] H.C. Debates, 12 November 1970, col. 636.

an ally to be welcomed. Even with this prospect in view there were several things which the new Committee might be expected to do which had not been done before. It might increase the flow of information to the Government from outside Whitehall and Westminster, and increase the flow of information from the Government to the outside world. It might improve the quality of decisions through the inward flow of information and better explain the decisions to the public through the outward flow. The best practical hopes that could be held out for the Expenditure Committee were that it might help to improve the quality of Government decisions about public spending by providing new channels for communications to and from Government.

4 The Expenditure Committee at Work I: the Members

The original recommendation for an Expenditure Committee proposed that it should consist of a general sub-committee and eight functional sub-committees each of nine members. However the Green Paper proposals, passed by the House of Commons in 1970, reduced the number to a General sub-committee and five functional sub-committees each of eight members making a total of forty-eight members in all. A chairman was put in over-all charge of the whole Committee. Unlike the Public Accounts Committee which is normally chaired by a prominent Opposition Member, the Expenditure Committee is chaired by a Member from the Government side. The first chairman was Edward du Cann, who soon resigned. His successor was Sir Henry D'Avigdor Goldsmid. Sir Henry remained in office till he retired from politics at the General Election in April 1974, since when the chairman has been James Boyden. The chairman is ex-officio a member of all sub-committees but he is not an active participant in any of them. In many ways his role is less significant than the role of the individual sub-committee chairmen, for they are the ones who decide what the sub-committees are going to do and how they are going to operate.

From the first meetings in early 1971 until March 1976 a total of 130 M.P.s in all have at one time or another served on the Expenditure Committee, some for its entire life, others for as little as three days. The composition of the Expenditure Committee, like that of any Parliamentary Committee, is basically determined by the Whips, who advise the Committee of Selection which nominates M.P.s to the various Committees. There are two ways by which a Member of Parliament may become a member of the Expenditure Committee. He may himself take the initiative and ask the Whips of his party to nominate him. Very often he will express an interest in joining a particular sub-committee. This sort of initiative is likely to occur either at the start of a new Parliament, when the Committee is being composed and when Members already in Parliament may wish to change their committee assignments and new Members may seek particular positions to suit their interests, or when a new Member enters Parliament as a result of a by-election. Many Members, however, find their way on to the Expenditure Committee, as they find their way on to other Parliamentary committees, because a vacancy has occurred and the Whips have to fill it. If a Member is promoted to Government office, dies, or takes up some other important committee assignment, the Whips approach other Members to ask if they are willing to fill the vacancy. They act, where they can, in accordance with Members' stated preferences. Their problem is that some sub-committees of the Expenditure Committee are over-subscribed and easy to fill but others are not so popular.

When the Expenditure Committee was first established, its membership was composed anew at the start of each yearly session of Parliament. There were a number of disadvantages attached to this method of determining the membership. The Parliamentary session very often did not commence until November and the composition of the many Select and Standing Committees was not finally determined until some time after the start when the Whips and the Leader of the House had agreed upon the sessional flow of business. When the membership of a Select Committee was not decided until a few weeks before Christmas, it was unlikely to get down to any serious work until after the Christmas recess. Then it found that its busiest time coincided with the busiest part of the Parliamentary year when the House was occupied with the committee stages of major legislation and with the Finance Bill. This compression of the Expenditure Committee's work did not help a rational allocation of Members' time. Since 1974 the Expenditure Committee has had its membership determined for the entire life of the Parliament. Some Committee members appointed in November 1974 are still serving without a break in June 1977. The practice of appointing the Committee for the whole Parliament should in theory ensure greater continuity of membership, but Members still move on and off the Committee during the course of a Parliament whenever they acquire new commitments, are promoted to Government office, resign from Parliament or die. In fact there has been more movement on and off some sub-committees between 1974 and 1977 than between 1971 and 1974. A practical consideration taken into account when the decision was made to appoint the Committee for the whole Parliament was that sub-committees would now be able to develop a greater continuity in their work and spread the work load more evenly over the Parliamentary year. The decision has had the effect of encouraging them to collect evidence over a number of sessions before producing a report. They have been able to engage in enquiries in greater depth than would be possible were they forced to compress their evidence sessions with witnesses into the months between Christmas and the summer recess.

Little real effort is made by the Whips to ensure that the Members appointed to the sub-committees are experts in the field covered by that sub-committee. The main criterion for appointment is willingness to serve. The Whips find it easy to fill vacancies on some sub-committees but difficult to keep others at full strength. They generally make little attempt to 'pack' sub-committees with men of particular views. However Members of known left-wing views are effectively excluded from membership of the Defence and External Affairs sub-committee. The reason suggested for this bias is that this sub-committee is allowed to see documents up to and including the category 'secret' (Members do not have access to documents marked 'most secret') which could not be made available to extreme left-wingers, who might be suspect on security grounds.[1] Because this bar excludes Members who are the most likely to call for cuts in defence spending, it is clear that the sub-committee has a built-in bias in favour of the defence services it oversees. One other sub-committee seems to some extent 'packed', perhaps because of the chairman's views. The composition of the Employment and Social Services sub-committee, chaired by left-winger Mrs Renée Short, has included a considerable number of Tribune group members.

None of the other sub-committees has exhibited any particular bias in the political interests of its members. There is no evidence that the membership of the Expenditure Committee is comprised of any particular category of Members; that is, it does not represent a special sub-group of the membership of the Whole House. The proportion of M.P.s with experience in the Committee who, in the change of Government in 1974, attained ministerial office was exactly the same as the proportion from among the victorious party as a whole. The Expenditure Committee from 1970 to 1974 was not therefore a nest of 'high fliers'. Neither has it been a repository for tired ex-Ministers, although there are a number of ex-Ministers among the membership. It contains both the 'professional' M.P.s who have little else to occupy

[1] The comments on membership are based on interviews with Expenditure Committee members who were asked how they obtained membership of the Committee. For details of interviews see Appendix A.

them except Parliamentary work, and M.P.s who simultaneously serve as directors of major British companies, journalists, barristers, etc.

Turnover

It is possible to gauge the popularity of the various sub-committees by showing the numbers of members serving on each during the periods 1971-April 1974 and November 1974-March 1977. The most popular sub-committees are those where the turnover is least and the membership is relatively stable. The least popular are those which have suffered from a constantly changing membership. The most popular sub-committee is that on Defence and External Affairs. This may seem surprising in view of the extremely low turnout at Defence debates and in view of the fact that Defence is a subject on which few Members specialise. It has been pointed out above,[2] however, that the subject of Defence generates intense interest among a minority of M.P.s, and this may be the reason why members of the sub-committee rarely wish to resign from it. Another explanation for the popularity of the Defence sub-committee offered (during interviews) by members of several sub-committees was the fact that this particular sub-committee undertakes an unusual number of attractive trips abroad. Although other sub-committees may also travel to collect evidence, Defence and External Affairs is more likely to do it often. Even if the scope of British troops abroad declines, there are still all the embassies to visit. A further suggestion for the popularity of the Defence sub-committee is that members get satisfaction from the fact that they have access to classified material. It gives them a feeeling of being near to the stuff of politics. However this suggestion perhaps needs qualification. Some Defence sub-committee members interviewed pointed out that the excessive classification of material in British Government was well recognised by them, and they got little satisfaction from seeing documents containing material classified as 'secret' by the British Government yet freely obtainable from other NATO sources. Another factor in the popularity of this particular sub-committee is the style of its chairman. He has held this post since the Expenditure Committee was first set up and is highly regarded by his committee members.

Apart from the period April to October 1974 the membership of the Defence sub-committee has been completely stable. Members once

[2] See above, pp. 35–36.

appointed have not left the sub-committee during the life of a Parliament. The chairman and two of the sub-committee members have served for the full period of six years, and one other member who had been on the General sub-committee from 1971 transferred to Defence when a vacancy occurred after the April 1974 election. The Members who were appointed in November 1974 replaced those who had lost their seats in the election that October, had given up their seats, or had become Ministers in the new Government. One of the original members of the Defence and Foreign Affairs sub-committee, James Boyden, became chairman of the Expenditure Committee in April 1974.

Next in terms of low turnover comes the Trade and Industry sub-committee. This sub-committee had only one replacement between 1971 and 1974 when Adam Butler was promoted to junior office and his place was taken by Richard Hornby. This sub-committee was popular with its members both under its original chairman, Bill Rogers, who became a Minister in 1974, and under Pat Duffy, who was its chairman from 1974 until he too became a junior Minister in 1976. This sub-committee has opted for enquiries of a rather political nature, but not subjects creating party political differences among the membership. Consequently it has been able to keep the political interests of its members alive without creating dissent among them. Members praised the way Bill Rogers handled the sub-committee, expressing approval of the way in which he allowed all members to participate fully in the committee's evidence sessions and deliberations. The sub-committee members have gained a certain amount of satisfaction from drawing attention to issues of a political nature which have aroused press and public interest, from their early enquiry into the wages and conditions of South African workers to their more recent enquiries into the British motor industry.

The Environment and Home Office (from 1974 Environment only) sub-committee has likewise enjoyed a relatively stable membership. Between 1971 and 1974 there were four changes of membership due in part to a change of chairmanship during that period. Since Arthur Jones undertook the chairmanship in 1974 the membership has been very stable with only two changes. One of these occurred when Timothy Sainsbury left the sub-committee to join the Select Committee on the Wealth Tax in which he played a major part. He returned to the Environment sub-committee when that assignment was completed. Only one member permanently relinquished his membership of the Environment sub-committee between 1974 and 1977.

Table One   Membership of the Expenditure Committee

	1970–Apr. 1974	Nov. 1974–Nov. 1976	Changes Nov. 1976– Mar. 1977
1. Members serving on the Expenditure Committee			
Defence	8	8	—
Trade and Industry	9	10	1
Environment and Home Office	12	9	1
Employment and Social Services	12	14	4
General	14	11	1
Education and Arts	15	12	1
2. Average turnover per session			
Defence	nil	nil	
Trade and Industry	¼	1	
Environment and Home Office	1	½	
Employment and Social Services	1	3	
General	1½	1½	
Education and Arts	1¾	2	

The General sub-committee has had a rather varied experience with membership turnover which has been much affected by the personality of the chairmen and the types of subject which they have chosen. At the start of 1971 the General sub-committee appeared to some members to hold out prospects of much interesting work, and the Whips found it over-subscribed. But when those appointed discovered the sort of enquiries which the then chairman, Dick Taverne, was trying to pursue, they found the style and content of the proceedings difficult to take and lost interest. When Taverne resigned the chairmanship, following his departure from the Labour Party, Robert Sheldon took it over. Sheldon did not however have long enough at the task before the April 1974 election to develop his own style. On the return to power of the Labour Party in 1974 he became a Minister, and the chairmanship of the General sub-committee passed to Michael English, who has held the post since that date. English has altered the direction of the sub-committee away from the highly technical subjects tackled by Taverne towards the role of a Select Committee on Economic Affairs. The sub-committee has attracted a lot of attention under his chairmanship both for its enquiries into topics such as inflation and the balance of payments and for its investigations into the processes by which decisions about public spending are made. The ability to attract attention from the press greatly enhances a committee's appeal, for it helps to give members the idea that they are doing something useful through their membership. The actual figures of turnover on the General sub-committee have not improved since the 1970–74 Parliament, but there are some particular reasons for the numbers of subsequent changes. In May 1974 one member, Maurice Edleman, died and was replaced by John Garrett. Nigel Lawson left the sub-committee in November 1976 to become an Assistant Whip.

The two sub-committees with the highest turnover rates are Employment and Social Services (to which Home Office was added in 1974), and Education and Arts. Between 1971 and April 1974 12 members served on the Employment and Social Services sub-committee, while between November 1974 and March 1977—a shorter period—the number of serving members rose to 18. This gives the sub-committee an average turnover rate of one member per session from 1971 to 1974 and of 6 members per session for the period 1974–77 (assuming that the figures for membership changes remain the same for the whole 1976–77 session as they are for November 1976–March 1977 only). The high turover rate cannot be related solely to the actual topics investigated. It is also due to the style of the chairman who has chosen to surround herself with, or has managed to attract to membership, mainly left-wingers of her party. This has not endeared the sub-committee to its Conservative members, some of whom are right-wing. It is always easier in a Select Committee to develop harmonious relations and to create a consensual style of decision making if the group's members are not too far apart in their general outlook on politics. But if some members have too pronounced or fixed a view, then it becomes harder to persuade other members with a different point of view to move towards a middle ground. It is clear that, in the case of the Employment sub-committee, the adversarial style has resulted in an increasing loss of interest among some members and a falling off in attendance. Between November 1974 and March 1977

11 Conservatives[3] and 7 Labour members served on it. There is no reason for believing that so long as the Labour side of this sub-committee is predominantly left-wing, the attractiveness of membership will increase.

In general terms therefore turnover on the sub-committees is related to various factors which combine together to make an attractive or an unattractive committee assignment. The personality of the chairman and his or her ability to get on well with the members is obviously important, for the sub-committee does to a large extent take its style and mode of political operation from its leader. His ability to prevent party differences intruding and to bring members together for agreed reports is essential to the long-term cohesion of the committee. Important too is the type of subject which the sub-committee decides to tackle. Many Members interviewed said that they liked subjects with 'political sex appeal'. Worthy subjects like some of those examined by the Environment sub-committee have an intellectual interest but little political attraction. A clear sense of direction, and a sense of success that derives as much from the feeling that reports are drawing the attention of the generality of M.P.s, of the quality press and of the informed public, as from direct impact on Government policy, also affects the ability of a sub-committee to keep its membership. Members who get some sort of feedback from their efforts are more likely to exert themselves in their Expenditure Committee work and to stick to it.

Expertise

Since the Expenditure Committee is divided into subject sub-committees and has taken upon itself the task of reviewing in depth particular functions of Government, an observer might imagine that a certain amount of expertise among its members would be helpful in its work of investigation. Members who have knowledge of a subject can guide enquiries along fruitful paths and make the most of their opportunities to examine witnesses in the evidence sessions. Expertise, however, does not appear to be a major qualification for appointment to the Expenditure Committee. This can be demonstrated by an examination of the previous experience and careers of the Members serving on it.

In order to facilitate the examination and measure the degree of

[3] One of the Conservatives, however, gave up his membership due to ill-health.

expertise in the various sub-committees, Members have been divided into the classifications of 'expert' and 'non-expert'. Members have been classed as 'expert' if there is any evidence at all in their backgrounds to indicate that they would bring to their work on the Expenditure Committee any previous experience useful during the course of the Committee's investigations. Such experience includes their education, occupation, membership of party committees or previous Government office. This method of classification tends to overestimate the degree of expertise among Members for two reasons. Firstly, some Members have only a scant knowledge of a subject and others have very considerable knowledge. It is not possible to tell from printed information about a man's experience how well informed he is. A degree in Economics does not ensure that a Member appointed to the General sub-committee has any idea of, say, methods of Treasury forecasting or control of public spending. His training may not even have given him the background necessary to become expert in such fields. The method of calculating expertise used here, however, assigns expertise both to the man who has never used his degree in Economics and to the man who has used it during his career as financial journalist or academic. Secondly, it is a fact that the investigations of the broad functional sub-committees can delve into the operations of several Government Departments. Members classed as 'expert' in one field within a sub-committee's competence may be laymen in another.

In spite of these problems of over-estimation of the degree of expertise, the results of a classification of Members into 'expert' and 'non-expert' do not indicate a high level of expertise on most sub-committees. Trade and Industry is the one exception. The figures for all other sub-committees contrast unfavourably with those for some of the 'Crossman' specialist committees established in 1966. Almost all of the members of the 1966 Education and Science Select Committee had previous experience as teachers, lecturers, or Government Ministers, and the Agriculture Committee was composed almost exclusively of Members from rural constituencies, farmers, land agents, etc. By contrast, a great many members of the Expenditure Committee (like the members of the previous Estimates Committee which the Expenditure Committee replaced) must be regarded basically as 'lay critics' of the Executive.

While many Members are far from expert in the subjects of their sub-committees at the time they are appointed, they can acquire a degree of expertise during their period of service. Many Members say

Table Two   Percentage of Expenditure Committee Members Classed as Expert

	1971–74	*1974–76*
Trade and Industry	90	82
Defence	75	38
Environment and Home Office	50	40
Education and Arts	40	50
General	38	38
Employment and Social Services	33	20

that the facts that they learn about Government provide one of the attractions of Expenditure Committee work. They feel that they are becoming experts by exposure to witnesses and memoranda. Some sub-committees have a number of very long serving members who have built up considerable experience of their subjects. There are three members of the Defence and External Affairs sub-committee who have been on that sub-committee since its inception, one of these being the chairman who had previous knowledge of Defence (Col. Sir Harwood Harrison). Two of the members of the Trade and Industry sub-committee have served since 1971, and Mrs Renée Short has been chairman of Employment and Social Services since that date. The advantage of long service as a source of expertise is that it enables members to recall previous enquiries and use the information gained in earlier years. The disadvantage of becoming an expert through this route is that the Expenditure Committee tends to draw its information from a relatively narrow range of sources[4] and relies particularly heavily on the Government for information. Therefore expertise obtained solely through long service on the Committee is likely to be somewhat one-sided. The lack of an independently formed expertise among the members inhibits the full exercise of their critical faculties in their oversight of Government spending.

The two sub-committees with more than 50 per cent of their members classified as 'expert', Trade and Industry, and Defence and External Affairs, are also the two that have enjoyed the most stable

[4] See below, Chapter 6.

membership. Clearly M.P.s who know about these particular subjects are attracted to the sub-committees concerned as a forum in which to develop and use their skills. Two of the three sub-committees with the fewest experts are the two with the least stable membership. It is rather curious that so few of the Members of the House of Commons with expertise in Education seek membership of the Education and Arts Sub-Committee. It may be that the relatively low-key, apolitical approach adopted by both chairmen of that sub-committee, Neil Marten from 1971 to 1974, and Janet Fookes since 1974, fails to appeal to most of those interested in Education (a topic on which there are strong ideological views). There are, according to many M.P.s, few among their number knowledgeable about the Arts; but the fact that one of those who is has chosen to become a member of the Environment sub-committee probably reflects the lack of attention paid by the Education and Arts sub-committee to the Arts side of its terms of reference. It failed, for example, to make an enquiry into the Mentmore Towers affair, which might have attracted some interest among Members of the House. It may also seem surprising that so few experts are attracted to membership of the Employment and Social Services sub-committee, since many M.P.s know a good deal about these subjects. It is, in contrast to Education and Arts, perhaps the over-political approach of the chairman that has discouraged experts from exercising their skills in this particular Parliamentary arena.[5] A chairman who wishes to build up a stable and expert sub-committee needs to tread a middle ground avoiding the development of party political clashes while at the same time maintaining his committee members' interest in their work.

When the minutes of evidence of the various sub-committees are analysed, several consequences of the relatively low levels of expertise may be observed. These include a failure to understand the subject matter, weak probing of the witnesses, an inability to undertake a thorough search for evidence (members of the sub-committees usually take little part in the selection of witnesses and leave control of the sources of information to the chairman, clerk, and specialist adviser if there is one), and enhancement of the role of specialist adviser to whom members may defer. One specialist adviser was asked at interview whether the sub-committee members would understand the very technical paper he was preparing for them. He replied that in the

[5] Several members interviewed indicated that a 'political' approach to Select Committee work discouraged some of their number.

main the members were unlikely to understand his memorandum but that that mattered little since he was more interested in how the Department would respond to it. This example shows how easy it is for members lacking expertise to be used as tools or as a vehicle through which outside bodies or individuals can seek to influence the Government.

The lack of expertise has several effects upon the questioning of witnesses during the evidence sessions. A close reading of the evidence sessions shows how often a line of questioning is broken too soon. One member may begin to probe a witness with a sequence of questions when another member chips in pushing the line of enquiry off at a tangent. To have four or five members, some of whom know little about the subject, question an expert witness is to give the advantage to that witness. Witnesses are able to tell the sub-committee what they want to hear. This is particularly true of civil service witnesses who are well briefed before their appearance yet do not have to face sustained cross examination from sub-committee members. The latter do not have the advantage of an expert who sits behind them guiding them as to what questions should be put. Some specialist advisers do offer members guidance in the general line of questioning in advance, but their role is limited by the fact that there is only one adviser per committee of eight members. A curious example of the way in which expertise can be useful to a committee member occurred during the questioning of I.C.I. witnesses in the Trade and Industry sub-committee during its 1974 enquiry into the wages and conditions of South African workers. One member, Mark Hughes, pursued an unusually penetrating line of questioning of the medical witnesses about evidence of malnutrition among employees. He was able to draw a distinction between clinical and sub-clinical malnutrition and thus reveal that, although there might not be evidence of clinical malnutrition among workers, some were suffering from sub-clinical malnutrition. He already knew that there were two possible forms of malnutrition because his sister was a doctor and he had discussed the matter with her. He therefore came to the committee room sufficiently well briefed to draw out relevant information from the witnesses. Lack of such ability to draw out what is not at first sight obviously relevant information is a serious deficiency in the Expenditure Committee stemming from the limited expertise of its members and from the lack of expert back-up staff to brief them. Witnesses sometimes go into the committee room with certain ideas and information that they wish to reveal and with other ideas that they wish to hide. If a committee is to get to the heart of the matter under review, it must draw out of the witnesses all the relevant information. It cannot do this unless it knows what questions have to be asked. Knowledge and information are such valuable currency in political influence that lack of expertise and skill is a serious bar to successful scrutiny of the Government by the Expenditure Committee.

Attendance

It is one thing to appoint Members to the Expenditure Committee but another to get them to come along and sit right through its meetings. It is difficult to get all of them to participate actively and in a manner that makes a positive contribution to the proceedings. Full participation in the Expenditure Committee requires the Member to take on a certain burden of work.

It is possible to get some idea of the burden of work which membership of the Expenditure Committee entails from the total number of meetings that a member of a sub-committee could attend. There are three types of meeting. The most important and onerous are the evidence sessions at which witnesses are orally examined. If the members are to prove effective examiners, they must do some preparation before the session. They need to read any memoranda provided by the witnesses and other relevant background information necessary for their understanding of the subject. The amount and quality of their general preparation and participation in the Committee's work can be judged to a large extent from the published minutes of evidence (any classified material presented to the Defence and External Affairs sub-committee appears as asterisks). Secondly, there are deliberative meetings. These take place in the first instance where the sub-committee is planning its work at the start of the Parliamentary year; short meetings may also be held before the evidence sessions to plan the line of questioning or to discuss future witnesses, and longer meetings are held at the end of an inquiry when the chairman's draft report and any other draft reports are examined and voted upon. The number of the final deliberative meetings to consider the report and the burden which these meetings place on Members varies with the length and complexity of the report and with the degree of partisanship in the sub-committee—that is, the extent to which the report is contested. Generally one or two deliberative sessions are sufficient to deal with a report, since the chairman's draft is usually accepted. Where a sub-committee takes on more than one subject in any one session, it will have, of course, an increased number of deliberative sessions. For technical reasons no records of these deliberative meetings are published. Sub-committees do not report direct to the House of Commons but to the whole Expenditure Committee which must consider and vote upon each report coming to it. The Expenditure Committee then reports to the House. Minutes of proceedings and records of votes in the Expenditure Committee, as a whole, are published. However, most reports pass through the whole Committee unamended and without a formal division and vote. Only if the sub-committees were able to report direct to the House, or were established independently of the whole Expenditure Committee as separate Select Committees, could the date of their deliberative sessions and any votes taken therein be published. As it is, we have no way of knowing how many deliberative sessions a sub-committee has held or what votes have been taken on its reports except from interviews with Members.

The third type of meeting, like the deliberative session, has no published records of proceedings. Sub-committees that travel outside Westminster to collect information occasionally have informal evidence sessions to gather material that may be used later in their report but is not printed in the minutes as formal evidence. The Defence and Foreign Affairs sub-committee has frequently collected information in this manner during travels to British Service installations at home and abroad, and to Embassies. The Trade and Industry sub-committee collected informal evidence from managers, shop stewards, and workers during its visits to motor vehicle factories in Britain and Europe in 1975. In 1977 the General sub-committee paid a visit to Washington to study—for its general information rather than for a special report —U.S. methods of controlling Federal Government spending. Because of such meetings for which there are no published records, it is only possible to provide a rough guide to the burden of work of Members from the printed evidence. It should be remembered however that formal evidence sessions are by far the most onerous and numerous of the meetings which committee members attend.

Table Three shows that there is some variation in the burden of work among the sub-committees, although for most the average number of evidence sessions has been one per week for the duration of the Parliamentary year. The variation in the number of meetings (apart from the first session 1970–71) is related to the fact that each sub-committee has a high degree of autonomy over the style and method of its enquiries. It is also related to the type of subject which the sub-committee has chosen to study. Some sub-committees have

Table Three   Number of Meetings (Formal Oral Evidence Sessions Only)

	1970–71	1971–72	1972–73	1973–74	Apr. 1974– Oct. 1974	1974–75	1975–76	Average per year
Trade and Industry	14	14	31	1	3	22	26	16
Defence and External Affairs	12	48	4	12	2	13	25	17
Employment and Social Services	—	52	19	5	10	12	25	21
Environment and Home Office	—	35	16	24	2	35	42	25
Education and Arts	11	20	17	—	3	14	18	14
General	8	12	5	2	8	7	33	12
Average	7	30	15	7	5	17	28	

Note (1) Meetings are recorded for the session in which they took place, not for the session in which the relevant report appeared.

(2) In session 1974 there were seven sub-committees. The figures have been recorded with those of the relevant permanent sub-committees.

undertaken large-scale, wide-ranging enquiries requiring evidence to be collected from a large number of witnesses during many meetings. Other sub-committees have undertaken small-scale, more technical enquiries for which the sources of information are relatively limited. In the case of the General sub-committee, for example, the increased number of meetings held in the session 1975–76 is due to change in the nature of its work. In its earlier days it was mainly concerned with technical aspects of the presentation and content of the Annual Expenditure White Papers, for which it required few meetings with witnesses. Since Michael English became chairman in 1974, it has extended its interests to wider economic issues for which it has to examine substantial amounts of evidence from a variety of sources.

Accurate measurement of attendances at Select Committee meetings is difficult because members come and go from the room and may attend for only a few minutes of a session lasting two hours or more. Even the shortest stay in the committee room ensures that a member is recorded as being present. Members arrange among themselves and with the chairman who is to come to particular sessions if, as generally happens, they cannot all be there. Sometimes the arrangements break down and too few Members turn up. This has unfortunate consequences, for unless three Members are present an evidence session cannot proceed. The problem of ensuring sufficient attendance at Select Committees has grown in recent years as the number of these Committees has expanded and as the amount of legislative work before the House has increased. Since the Standing Committee system must be serviced from the same pool of Members who also service the Select Committees, a heavy burden such as that in the first three annual sessions of the November 1974 Parliament makes adequate and full attendance at the Expenditure Committee most difficult. Members have sometimes found themselves scheduled to sit in two committees at one and the same time, with the result that they have had to dodge in and out of the respective committee rooms paying flying visits to vote or ask a question as the case might be.

Table Four shows the actual levels of attendance at sub-committee meetings. Attendances have been generally around the 70 per cent mark, but there has been some variation. Trade and Industry, Defence and General, have enjoyed consistently high attendance, while Environment and Home Office, and Education and Arts, have experienced much lower levels. Employment and Social Services suffered a particularly marked decline in average attendances from the first session of 1970–71 until 1974 but thereafter increased. Attendance does not seem to be related to the number of meetings that a sub-committee has. Even where the burden of work in terms of meetings is great, as in the case of the Trade and Industry sub-committee, attendances can be high. In the period 1970–74 Trade and Industry had both the highest number of meetings and the highest percentage rate of attendance. But attendance does seem related to the popularity of a sub-committee and the degree of expertise among its membership. The sub-committee with the highest percentage attendance, Trade and Industry, was a popular sub-committee with a low turnover of members. It also had the highest number of members with previous expertise. Attendance was lowest in Education and Arts and Environment and Home Office both of which had a high turnover of membership and few members with previous expertise. If, for any reason whether it be the nature of the subject studied or the personality of the chairman, members do not enjoy their work, they first show their lack of enthusiasm by becoming poor attenders of meetings. Eventually they leave the sub-committee for some other more attractive assignment. Therefore it seems clear that the burden of work

Table Four   Levels of Attendance*

	1970–71†	1971–72	1972–73	1973–74	1974	1974–75	1975–76
Trade and Industry	—	$\frac{198}{224}$	—	$\frac{231}{272}$	$\frac{18}{21}$	$\frac{146}{176}$	$\frac{148}{184}$
Defence	—	$\frac{256}{336}$	$\frac{52}{69}$	$\frac{42}{56}$	$\frac{11}{14}$	$\frac{143}{192}$	$\frac{75}{104}$
Employment and Social Services	—	$\frac{70}{96}$	$\frac{157}{224}$	$\frac{44}{88}$	$\frac{48}{70}$	$\frac{65}{96}$	$\frac{146}{200}$
Environment and Home Office	—	$\frac{71}{104}$	$\frac{193}{304}$	$\frac{58}{80}$	$\frac{10}{14}$	$\frac{94}{128}$	$\frac{98}{168}$
Education and Arts	$\frac{63}{88}$	—	$\frac{116}{160}$	$\frac{93}{136}$	$\frac{15}{18}$	$\frac{70}{104}$	$\frac{90}{162}$
General	$\frac{54}{64}$	$\frac{73}{96}$	$\frac{21}{24}$	$\frac{5}{8}$	$\frac{41}{49}$	$\frac{24}{32}$	$\frac{176}{240}$

* (The figures are actual attendances over possible attendances)

Note: Figures refer to years in which reports are published, not to years in which meetings actually took place.

	Percentage Attendance	
	1970–74	1974–76
Trade and Industry	86	82
General	79	75
Defence	76	74
Education and Arts	71	62
Employment and Social Services	66	70
Environment and Home Office	64	65

Table Five   Percentage Evidence Sessions Attended 1970–74

	Conservative	*Labour*
Defence and External Affairs	95	73
Environment and Home Office	68.5	60
Employment and Social Services	54	68
General	92.3	92
Trade and Industry	80.6	87.4
Education and Arts	81.2	51.8

which membership of the Expenditure Committee imposes is more willingly borne if members value their association with a sub-committee and wish to remain on it, and if they feel that its work is relevant to their interests.

There is also some variation of attendance at sub-committees according to the party of the member. As Table Five above shows, Conservatives have been higher attenders on Defence and External Affairs, Environment and Home Office, and General, while Labour members have been more regular attenders at the other sub-committees.

The difference in attendance rate according to party seems to be related to the party of the sub-committee chairman, for Conservatives attended more regularly than Labour members those sub-committees with Conservative chairmen and vice versa. The one exception to this pattern was the General sub-committee in which there was practically no variation of attendance among the parties.

Participation

It is not possible to devise an absolutely precise measure for participation in the work of the Expenditure Committee for the reason, given above, that no printed information is available concerning what happens in the deliberative and informal evidence sessions of its sub-committees. In fact this matters little since the member who takes small part in the examination of witnesses but plays an active role during consideration of the report is, according to members of the Expenditure Committee and its clerks, extremely rarely found in that Committee. Such unusual behaviour is more likely to be found, if at all, in a Select Committee which is considering a highly political subject and which is set up for that one enquiry only. In such circumstances a few members may come to their work with their minds already made up as to the recommendations which they wish to see in the Committee's report, and may not think that it matters what the evidence says. In the Select Committee on the Wealth Tax (1975), for example, a number of members from the Labour side scarcely participated at all in the examination of witnesses but came along to the final deliberative sessions to ensure that the report conformed to their views.[6] In the Expenditure Committee the nature of the subjects chosen for enquiry, the style adopted by most chairmen, and the fact that members need to get on with one another if they are to continue to work together for a long period in the same small group, mean that members must keep to the norm of producing reports related to the evidence. M.P.s who feel that Select Committee reports need not conform to the evidence presented do not feel comfortable on the Expenditure Committee, and those M.P.s of this category who have tried the work soon leave to find more obviously 'political' activity. In general, Expenditure Committee members who perform actively in its published evidence sessions are also active in its other deliberative and informal meetings. Because this is the case, the evidence sessions may be taken as a reasonable guide to the average rates of participation among members.

Just as it is not possible to be absolutely precise as to the amount of participation in all committee activities, so it is not possible to provide much indication in numerical terms of the quality of a member's participation. That can only be gauged by a careful reading of the questions asked by members and the responses to them. All that can be done by measurement is to provide a crude indication of the amount of participation in terms of how many questions, on average, a member asks. Participation is measured by counting the number of questions asked by a member during the course of an enquiry and then dividing that total by the number of times he had attended sub-committee meetings. If this measurement is taken over a large number of enquiries and sub-committees, general patterns of participation emerge which can then be related to other facts known about the sub-committees such as their stability of membership, rate of attendance, and the degree of expertise among members.

Participation scores have been calculated for all sub-committees in the years 1970–74 and these appear as a set of diagrams in Table Six. In addition, scores have been calculated for a number of individual enquiries conducted during the years 1975–76 and 1976–77. The patterns prevailing in 1970–74 were found to recur in the later period.

---

[6] In the event there was so much political dispute in the Committee that members could not agree on a report. Instead they produced five separate draft reports.

Table Six

In each chart, the average number of questions asked at each meeting is measured on the vertical axis, and the number of members of the committee measured on the horizontal axis.

GENERAL

━━━Participation score of chairman

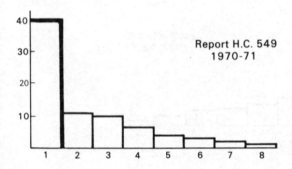

Report H.C. 549
1970-71

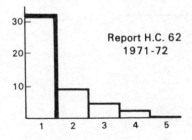

Report H.C. 62
1971-72

GENERAL—continued

■ Participation score of chairman

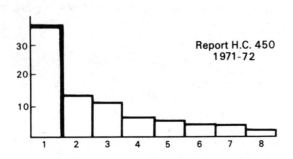

Report H.C. 450
1971-72

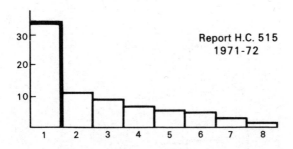

Report H.C. 515
1971-72

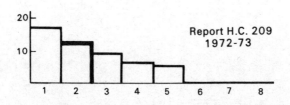

Report H.C. 209
1972-73

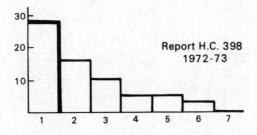

Report H.C. 398
1972-73

DEFENCE AND EXTERNAL AFFAIRS

━━━ Participation score of chairman

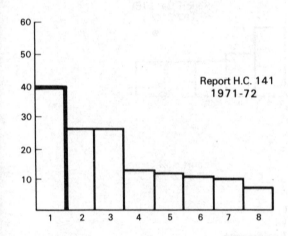

Report H.C. 141
1971-72

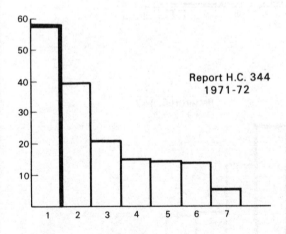

Report H.C. 344
1971-72

DEFENCE AND EXTERNAL AFFAIRS—continued

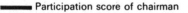
Participation score of chairman

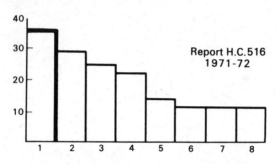

Report H.C.516
1971-72

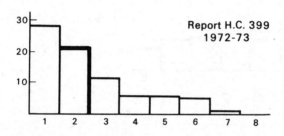

Report H.C. 399
1972-73

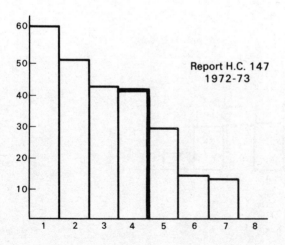

Report H.C. 147
1972-73

DEFENCE AND EXTERNAL AFFAIRS—continued

■ Participation score of chairman

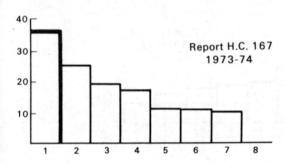

Report H.C. 167
1973-74

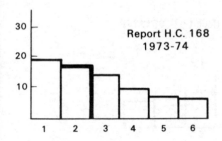

Report H.C. 168
1973-74

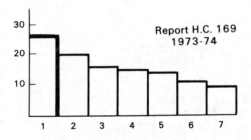

Report H.C. 169
1973-74

TRADE AND INDUSTRY

—— Participation score of chairman

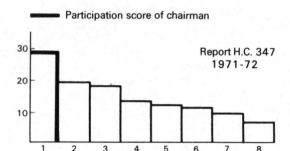

Report H.C. 347
1971-72

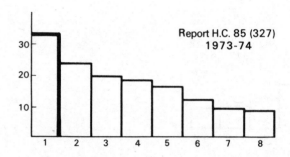

Report H.C. 85 (327)
1973-74

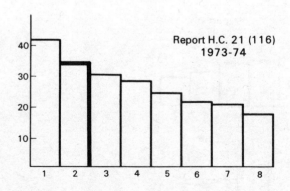

Report H.C. 21 (116)
1973-74

EDUCATION AND ARTS

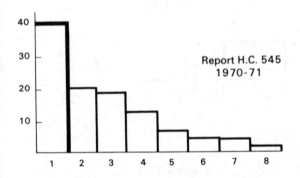

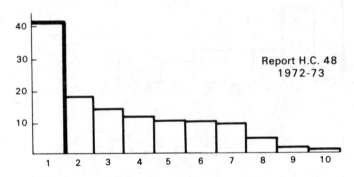

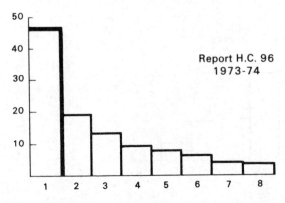

ENVIRONMENT AND HOME OFFICE

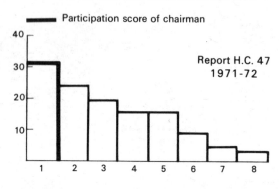

Report H.C. 47
1971-72

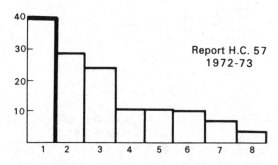

Report H.C. 57
1972-73

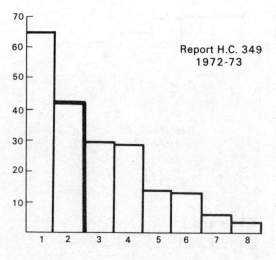

Report H.C. 349
1972-73

EMPLOYMENT AND SOCIAL SERVICES

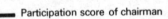 Participation score of chairman

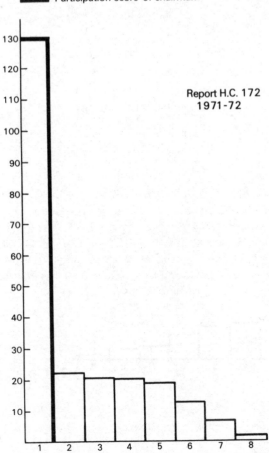

Report H.C. 172
1971-72

EMPLOYMENT AND SOCIAL SERVICES—continued

Participation score of chairman

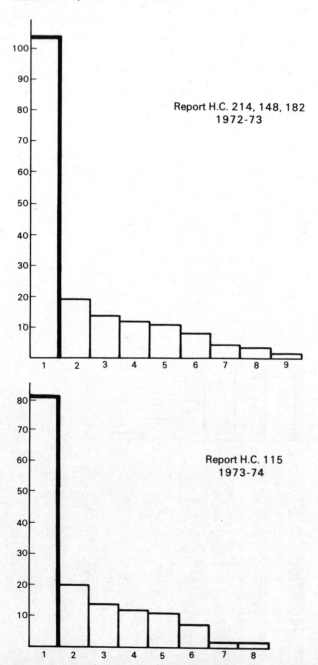

Report H.C. 214, 148, 182
1972-73

Report H.C. 115
1973-74

The diagrams show that there are three distinct patterns of participation: normal, even, and chairman dominant. The normal pattern of participation is where the chairman, taking the leadership role, is generally somewhat more active than the other members of the sub-committee, and where he is supported by one or two other reasonably active members. The remainder of the sub-committee trails behind as low participators. In the even participation model there is little variation of participation among the members of the sub-committee including the chairman. The chairman may not, in all enquiries, ask the greatest number of questions; this leadership role may be taken by another member. In the even participation examples, however, the chairman is among those members with the higher range of scores. The third type of participation patterns is that of chairman dominant. In this type the chairman is noticeably the leader in the Committee's work, taking the lion's share of the questioning of the witnesses and often asking more than twice as many questions as the next most active member.

Table Six reveals too that there is variation of participation patterns along three dimensions. The pattern may vary from enquiry to enquiry, from sub-committee to sub-committee, and from chairman to chairman. There seem however to be persistent patterns of participation for each sub-committee so long as it retains the same chairman. The variation in participation appears to be explained more by the sub-committee and its chairman than by the nature of the subject investigated.

Most of the enquiries by the Environment and Home Office sub-committee and the General sub-committee under the chairmanship of Robert Sheldon fell into the category of normal distribution of participation. Although the chairman led the committee, he did not dominate its proceedings to the exclusion of others. These sub-committees had few experts to take over a leadership role, so the chairman filled it. Most enquiries by Defence and External Affairs, and Trade and Industry, fell into the category of even participation. But the distribution of participation here varied from enquiry to enquiry and even from meeting to meeting according to the type of witness being questioned. Expertise seems to be an important factor in the even participation model, as exemplified by these sub-committees. In the Trade and Industry sub-committee between 1970–74 one member, Adam Butler, a Director of Courtaulds, participated on average only slightly less than the chairman, and another active participant was Joel Barnett, an accountant. We still find particular members playing an active role in this sub-committee after 1974. This has clearly been the case with Robert Maxwell Hyslop, once an engineer with Rolls Royce, who dominated many of the meetings of the Trade and Industry sub-committee during its enquiry into the motor vehicle industry. He was most at home questioning the expert witnesses. Other members with experience of industrial relations and factory conditions came into their own when the sub-committee turned for evidence to the trade unions and shop floor workers. Another pattern of participation is observed in other committee enquiries. The enquiries of the General sub-committee under the chairmanship of Dick Taverne, all the enquiries of the Employment and Social Services sub-committee (which has been chaired since its establishment by Renée Short) and, to a lesser extent, of the Education and Arts sub-committee under both of its chairmen, Neil Marten and Janet Fookes, come into the category of chairman dominant. In a number of investigations conducted by these sub-committees, the chairman has asked more than twice the number of questions asked by any other member. Participation by some members during these investigations has been at a very low level.

If the general over-all patterns of participation are related to the factors considered earlier in this chapter, some clear relationships can be observed. The more 'popular' sub-committees tend to have a normal or even pattern of participation, while the more 'expert' ones tend to have an even pattern of participation over-all, with particular differences related to individual members' expertise and interests. Where there is either normal or even participation, there is also a comparatively high level of popularity, stable membership, good attendance at meetings and a reasonable level of expertise. Where there is a dominant chairman, there tends to be unstable membership, poor attendance, and lack of expertise. Which are causes and which are effects is not clear, but these characteristics are clustered together in such a way as to make it appear that members neither work hard, nor particularly enjoy being on a sub-committee with a dominant chairman. The role of the chairman is obviously a crucial factor in determining the success of failure of a sub-committee.

Rewards

Members of the Expenditure Committee can be divided into four categories on the basis of their participation in its work. First come the sub-committee chairmen. While some chairmen are undoubtedly more active than others, it is the case that as a group they are the most active members devoting the greatest amount of time and effort to the Committee. The second category is that of 'experts'. These members join because they wish to use their expertise in one or other of the sub-committees. They can be extremely important and active during enquiries related to their own interests, but may be less active if and when their sub-committee studies a topic which they know little about. Members of the third category may be called the 'politicos'. These are men who are active in whatever Parliamentary arena they find themselves. They include the sort of M.P. who asks a great number of Parliamentary questions and takes pains to be in the House for important events and speak and interject as often as possible. They may know absolutely nothing about the topic studied by their sub-committee and may not necessarily do much homework to acquaint themselves with it, but they do ask a large number of questions from the witnesses. Politicos who take the trouble to work at their Expenditure Committee enquiries can contribute to its reports. Finally come the 'sleepers', members put on to the Committee mainly to make up its numbers. They participate little and cannot be said to add more than the occasional thought to a sub-committee's final recommendation.

Why do Members of Parliament join the Expenditure Committee and what rewards do they get for any effort they put into its work? The answers to this question can only be tentative. Those suggested here have been obtained primarily from interviews held with the Members themselves.[7] Clearly M.P.s have a number of conflicting goals towards which their daily work is directed, some of these being particularly relevant to the Expenditure Committee and others less so. One major goal for M.P.s in the British Parliamentary system is that of political advancement. The House of Commons is the route to executive position. There is no other way to it, except by membership of the House of Lords. But the Expenditure Committee is not an avenue recognised as leading to high office. A man who is able to display a chairman's skill in managing an Expenditure sub-committee will of course not do himself damage in the eyes of those promoting his career. If he is ambitious, however, he will probably find other more effective means of drawing attention to his ability. The kind of activity most required in a Select Committee—expert questioning of witnesses and the extraction of information—is not the sort that most attracts the attention of party managers. They are more likely

[7] See Appendix A for details of interviews with Expenditure Committee members. Where quotations are taken from these interviews they are referred to as 'Interview'. The author conducted the interviews on the understanding that individual members would not be named.

to be influenced by a successful speech on the floor of the House. It must also be recognised that party managers and leaders are not generally present at the Expenditure Committee to see a man in action. Because they do not attend Select Committee meetings, they do not have the opportunity personally to observe Members 'making their mark' as they do when Members are displaying their talents on the floor of the House. For these reasons the Expenditure Committee is not an important part of a would-be Minister's apprenticeship. A number of the Committee's members did attain office in 1974, and a few more of its members or ex-members have obtained junior Ministerial posts since that date, but their promotion cannot be related to anything they have done on the Committee. Indeed it is quite possible for Members who have attained a degree of expertise on a sub-committee later to be moved into Government or Opposition front-bench posts for which they have had no useful background experience. When Pat Duffy was plucked from the chairmanship of Trade and Industry in mid-enquiry, it was not to use his knowledge of the motor vehicle industry in a relevant Ministry but to place him in a junior position as Under Secretary for the Navy.

Another important goal for M.P.s is that of re-election. Since the average M.P. wishes to keep in the good favours of his constituency party managers, he needs constantly to display to them and to the generality of his constituents that he is doing a good job at Westminster. This goal is not easily satisfied through membership of the Expenditure Committee, since the Committee's powers and procedure do not allow him to use it to promote particular and local causes. Active participation in the Committee is unlikely to commend itself to constituents in the same way as a speech on the floor of the House requesting higher spending on some local project. Select Committees rarely get noticed by local presses. Members say that their constituents do not know of the existence of the Expenditure Committee and that, even if they did, they would not have any appreciation of its function. Were the Committee to have the powers, like those of Congressional Committees, to recommend detailed changes in expenditure plans and to expect that they would be adopted, then it would probably become a focus for local pressures and for 'pork barrel' politics. But as it cannot make any changes to the Government's plans, it has no attraction as a channel for constituency demands.

Perhaps all M.P.s, before reaching the House of Commons, have a belief that their election will give them the chance to stamp their impress upon the Government machinery, either because they have the ambition to become a Cabinet Minister (and many do have that ambition) or because they believe that what they will say or do in the House will influence the course of events. Membership of the Expenditure Committee is only marginally useful in fulfilling this goal, perhaps because it is a goal that cannot in any case be easily attained from the backbenches. The belief that membership of the Committee will enable an M.P. to influence the Government offers only a partial explanation of the motives for membership and participation. Members can see for themselves after a while on the Committee just how marginal is its influence over the Government and public spending. Any M.P. who comes on to the Expenditure Committee with great hopes of altering Government policy by his recommendations is therefore likely to become disillusioned. Sub-committee chairmen are the most likely to retain some belief in the efficacy of their work, yet a few other Members, in spite of what they know about the response of Government to Select Committees in general, continue to exhibit a touching trust in the system. Most Members, however, become realistic in their evaluation of the relative lack of power over Government decisions which the Expenditure Committee possesses.

While major goals of M.P.s are unlikely to be achieved through Committee membership, some more prosaic goals can be fulfilled by this means. Most M.P.s enter the House expecting to be given something useful to do, even if they remain as backbenchers and do not gain Ministerial or Opposition front-bench positions. One function of the Expenditure Committee is that it provides an interest to occupy backbenchers. Many of its members have no further hopes (or great hopes) of office, and a number of them have no considerable outside activities to occupy their lives. Some are relative newcomers to the House who think that Expenditure will prove to be one of the more interesting Select Committees. Occasionally a Member quite freshly elected from a by-election makes his way immediately on to the Committee—as was the case with Robert Rhodes James, the winner of the 1976 by-election at Cambridge. Also, M.P.s (who in this respect behave like many other people) desire to make the most of any fringe benefits their job offers, and undoubtedly some of them enjoy going on such trips abroad as the Expenditure Committee may make. This however is a weak explanation to account for membership of any sub-committee save perhaps Defence and External Affairs, for few of them make frequent overseas visits and there are now many other Parliamentary delegations going abroad to satisfy those M.P.s with a desire to see the world. A minor additional objective of many M.P.s is to avoid too many unattractive committee duties. Acceptance of a place on the Expenditure Committee lessens the chance that the Whips will come along and ask a Member to take on some other, perhaps less interesting, task. A few of those in the category of 'sleepers' join the Expenditure Committee for just this reason.

Some M.P.s have, as one of their goals, the attainment of prestige in the eyes of other Members of the House, either generally, in which case they try to display their talents by making excellent or stirring speeches in the Chamber, or among particular groups of Members with whom they are associated, in which case they endeavour to develop special skills and knowledge. They feel flattered to have their colleagues and those whom they respect asking advice or seeking information from them. One of the attractions of the Expenditure Committee is that it enables its members to learn much about certain aspects of Government. The members appreciate the opportunities afforded by the Committee to increase their knowledge. As far as more general prestige is concerned, however, relatively little accrues to ordinary members of the Committee except perhaps to those on Defence and External Affairs. As a rule prestige is won through Select Committee work only by those who become chairmen. Perhaps the most prestigious position which a backbencher can hold is still the chairmanship of the Public Accounts Committee. The chairmanship of a popular and interesting sub-committee of the Expenditure Committee likewise confers an element of prestige on the holder of that office.

The Expenditure Committee, last of all, provides a useful arena for what might be called the 'maverick' politician who wishes to display the crusading spirit. This role is really only available to the sub-committee chairmen who have control of their committee's activities and choose what they want to study and how they will do it. If a chairman wishes to do so and is prepared to face the hard work and possible difficulties such a choice may entail, he can use the committee as a platform for the display of his investigatory powers. Examples of sub-committee chairmen who have used the Expenditure Committee in this way include Michael English, chairman of the General sub-committee since 1974, who saw in it the opportunity to provide the House of Commons with what is, in effect, a Select Committee on Economic Affairs, and Pat Duffy, who went out of his way to lead his sub-committee, Trade and Industry, along an obstacle-strewn path in investigating public spending on the motor vehicle industry.

All the goals of M.P.s considered above are external to the Committee itself and must be seen as only partial explanations of why they become members. It is clear that that body is not the only Parliamentary means whereby an M.P. can achieve his aims and that it provides relatively few rewards (fewer for ordinary members than for chairmen). While the external goals of members may to some degree explain why they join the Committee, they are not sufficient to explain why they remain on it once they have been appointed. It is necessary to look at the internal operation of the sub-committees to understand more fully why some members stay on it and others leave. As well as the fulfilment of their external goals members are encouraged to stay on the sub-committees and work hard on it firstly by the intrinsic interest of the subject matter. Many of them say that they like topics with 'political sex appeal'. What they mean by this is not clear, for some of them have more exalted ideas than others. The least that it means is that they expect their sub-committee to engage in investigations into subjects that will not send them to sleep during meetings. They have no wish for subjects that are too technical or difficult to understand, or that require too much preparation. They like subjects that will arouse a degree of interest among other Members of the House and among the general public. Issues of current interest such as the wages of South African workers have an obvious attraction for many of them; subjects such as New Towns or the form of the White Paper on Public Expenditure are less appealing. A second factor internal to the sub-committees themselves which determines membership is the degree of cohesion developed in the group. The leadership role of sub-committee chairmen has already been stressed. It is up to the chairman to develop a cohesive and non-partisan sub-committee on which M.P.s are likely to stay. If a Select Committee set up especially to study one particular subject disbands immediately its work is over, there is no obvious need to work in a non-partisan manner and create a spirit of cohesion. But if a Select Committee like the Expenditure Committee is to stay in operation with the same members over a number of years, then a high level of partisan behaviour is most undesirable. A sub-committee which wants to keep its members, to develop a sense of corporate spirit, and to produce agreed reports without too much trouble, will need to choose interesting topics and tackle them in a manner likely to encourage a bi-partisan approach.

5 The Expenditure Committee at Work II: the Topics

When the Expenditure Committee was first established, it was hoped that the work of its sub-committees would be co-ordinated and integrated into a programme of study of the annual Expenditure White Papers. These hopes were clearly expressed in the Report of the Procedure Committee which recommended the establishment of the Expenditure Committee.[1] The Procedure Committee proposed that the General sub-committee should be the co-ordinating body. It would select the members of the functional sub-committees and exercise in normal circumstances the functions of the main Committee including the presentation of the reports to the House. Furthermore it would examine the White Paper as a whole, while the functional sub-committees would examine those sections of the White Paper that fell within their terms of reference. The results of this co-ordinated study in depth of the White Paper were then supposed to be available to the House of Commons for its use during the White Paper debate. However, when the Expenditure Committee was set up in 1971, the General sub-committee was not given the co-ordinating role that the Procedure Committee had proposed. It was made equal in status with the other sub-committees. An additional informal steering group was established to guide the sub-committee's work, but it met only a few times and was abandoned during the very first session of the Expenditure Committee's operation. Not till the session 1976–77 were any further serious attempts made to get the sub-committees to spend at least part of their time examining those parts of the White Paper that fell within their competence. Such exercises were, and are, regarded as something to be done quickly, as an additional task to the sub-committee's normal enquiries and peripheral to the main substance of its work. The failure to adhere to a co-ordinated programme was due first of all to the fact that each chairman had his own ideas

[1] *Scrutiny of Public Expenditure and Administration*, H.C. 410, 1968–69.

about the role which his sub-committee should adopt and about the sort of enquiries he wanted to undertake. No chairman desired merely to carry out tasks assigned to him or become part of an integrated, planned scheme of enquiries. A second factor inhibiting the development of an integrated approach among the sub-committees was the failure of Governments to produce White Papers on Expenditure at the regular appointed time each year. The irregularity with which these have appeared renders a work plan based on co-ordinated examination of the Government's future policies impracticable. As a result of this failure to work in an integrated fashion, no one can really speak of '*the* Expenditure Committee' when discussing the details of its operations because there are in effect six sub-committees working as individual Expenditure Committees. Each is now more or less autonomous in the choice of subjects it investigates and each has developed its own style and methods of working.

The sub-committee chairman is generally the most influential member in the process of selecting the topics for enquiry. When a new chairman is appointed, he may take over a subject already agreed upon or even started by a previous chairman, or he may rely upon the clerk to supply him with a list of topics (perhaps one already drawn up under an earlier regime), or he may take up office with his own firm ideas regarding the subjects he wants his sub-committee to investigate. He may have close relationships with one or two other members of his sub-committee—generally the most active members— in which case the choice of future topics may be discussed with them. By and large however it is up to him to take the initiative in the choice of topics, and this choice in turn affects the whole style of the sub-committee's work. Only very occasionally does a chairman find that he is not able to persuade his colleagues to accept his suggested topic— as was the case with Neil Marten who wanted the Education and Arts sub-committee to investigate Education in the E.E.C. but found little enthusiasm for his idea.

A survey of the topics studied by the various sub-committees reveals the extent to which each has adopted its own style of operation and used the opportunities available. Both the General sub-committee and Defence and External Affairs have conducted a large number of enquiries (more than twenty each in five years). Some of these enquiries have been technical and small scale in scope, others have been broad and large scale. Under its first chairman the General sub-committee kept to technical and small-scale subjects such as the form and presentation, and to a lesser extent the content, of the

Expenditure White Papers. These enquiries were conducted as a dialogue between the sub-committee (mainly the chairman) with its specialist adviser on the one hand, and the Treasury on the other. But such narrow and technical subjects did not greatly appeal to the majority of sub-committee members, nor did they arouse much interest outside Parliament. Under its third chairman (the second stayed in office only a few months) in the period from 1974, this sub-committee edged its way towards the role of a Select Committee on Economic Affairs by picking topics of broad general economic concern such as *Public Expenditure and the Balance of Payments* and *The Financing of Public Expenditure*. In the session 1976–77 it began a large enquiry into the *Civil Service after Fulton*. This change of direction is the direct result of the chairman's particular interests. This is not to say that the General sub-committee has entirely relinquished its older role of examining narrow, technical aspects of public spending. It monitors the contents of successive Public Expenditure White Papers and Government announcements of changes in the level of public spending.[2] This work, which does not require elaborate collection of evidence, allows it to keep an eye on broad movements in actual spending plans, and complements the longer enquiries into the relationship between public spending and economic management which it conducts.

Like the General sub-committee the Defence and External Affairs sub-committee (which has had only one chairman between 1971 and 1977) has engaged in the practice of making both small-scale technical enquiries and broad surveys of public spending in its particular fields. It has been helped in its choice of topics by the fact that its terms of reference cover the work of just two Departments: Defence, which is extremely large, and the Foreign Office, which is extremely small. It began by concentrating on the more limited subjects such as *Nuclear Weapons*, *The Multi-Role Combat Aircraft*, *The Cruiser Programme*, *Defence Medical Services*, *Accommodation and Staffing in Ottawa and Washington* and *Service Married Quarters in Gibraltar*. In 1973–74 it made its first general survey of *Defence Expenditure* and it has since continued looking at over-all levels of spending in its fields by commenting on *The Defence Cuts* (1974), *The Defence Review Proposals*, (1974–75), *Defence* (1975–76) and *Defence Policy after the Review* (1975–76). The sub-committee initially held the view that it should accept the level of Defence spending as given and then see whether the public was getting value for money. This attitude was generally shared by all members of the sub-

[2] For the full details of each Report see Appendix B.

committee. But in later years they became concerned at the effects of large and frequent cuts and adjustments to the Defence budget and thus moved further and further into the area of questioning the general policy behind Defence spending. They have discovered too that general cuts often have particular results—such as rusting helicopters in Hong Kong, or pilots having to miss training flights for lack of aviation fuel.

It is thus clear from the choice of topics of both the General and Defence and External Affairs sub-committees that they have to some extent continued the practice of the old Estimates Committee by looking at value for money within a function of Government and at technical matters regarding the control of expenditure. But they have also, since 1974, branched out into wider enquiries satisfying those expectations of Members who thought that the Expenditure Committee could be more concerned with the development of policy at early stages. The other sub-committees have not yet developed this double aspect of their role. They have concentrated their efforts on detailed examination of specific items of spending, and have thus fulfilled the same general function as the Estimates Committee. Furthermore, each of them has managed about two enquiries per year, with the exception of Trade and Industry which has averaged only one. None therefore has conducted so many enquiries as either General or Defence and External Affairs.

The Education and Arts sub-committee has spent its time on Education, not on the Arts. Its first chairman took the view that Education was the more important aspect of its work in terms of need. Indeed, in its first four years it seemed to be firmly attached to examination only of the more costly sectors of education—namely, the post-school sector. Its three major studies before the 1974 elections were *Further and Higher Education, Postgraduate Education* and *Education Maintenance Allowances in the 16–18 Years Age Group.* On acquiring a new chairman in 1974, it altered the direction of its interests to study *Charity Commissioners and their Accountability, Priorities and Decision Making in the DES* and *The Attainments of the School Leaver.* The change in emphasis reflects, once again, the particular concerns of the new chairman, an ex-school teacher and ex-chairman of an Education Committee. Of all its enquiries only *Priorities and Decision Making in the DES* (a study of the planning and policy making process) could be regarded as a subject unlikely to have been studied within the terms of reference of the House's previous Estimates Committee machinery. The other topics have been quite specific and related to whether the country was obtaining 'value for money' from its spending on particular sectors of education. This sub-committee has carefully avoided the more political aspects of its subject matter.

Environment and Home Office (since 1974 Environment only) has also tended to avoid political subjects. Prior to the 1974 elections it studied *Probation and After Care, Urban Transport Planning, House Improvement Grants* and *Public Expenditure on Transport*, and it also began an enquiry into *New Towns* for which it took evidence over several sessions. Since 1974 it has examined *The Redevelopment of the London Dockland, National Parks and the Countryside* and *Planning Procedures*. Its investigations have therefore always been concerned with spending on specific items of Government and never with the question of over-all spending on the Environment.

The last two sub-committees, Employment and Social Services and Trade and Industry, have been the boldest in selecting topics of political interest. Employment and Social Services attempted political enquiries from the start. Its very first investigation concerned *National Health Service Facilities for Private Patients*. The Chairman chose the matter of pay beds in the NHS because she felt the issue of private medicine had disappeared from the forefront of Labour Party policy. Her idea was to show how pay beds harmed the NHS, so giving ammunition to those who wished to eliminate private practice from hospitals as soon as Labour attained office. This choice of topic got the sub-committee off to a bad start, for many of its members objected to the overtly political objectives behind the selection of the subject. The experience seems to have taught the sub-committee a lesson. With the exception of one later enquiry of 1975–76 into *DHSS Statistics*, it has not again gone into any subject which is on the face of it a straight 'political' enquiry. Save for a short study in 1974 of *Expenditure Cuts in Health and Personal Social Services* and a wider-ranging examination during 1975–77 of *Preventive Medicine*, its other enquiries have concerned specific items of expenditure. These have included studies of various aspects of Employment Services in the session 1972–73 and studies of *Accident and Emergency Services* (1973–74), *Police Recruitment and Wastage* (1974), and the *Children and Young Persons' Act* (1974–75).

Of all the sub-committees Trade and Industry has conducted the fewest enquiries, has covered the narrowest range of topics, and has continued, successfully, to examine subjects with a high degree of political interest. Its first two subjects were *Public Money in the Private Sector* (a general survey of its remit) and, as concomitant of the first subject, *Regional Development Incentives*. Then in the session 1973–74, it made a significant move by investigating *Wages and Conditions of African Workers Employed by British Firms in South Africa*. This enquiry marked a turning point in the ability of sub-committees to choose their own subjects. Trade and Industry's proposal of this investigation drew complaints from other backbenchers who thought that the subject lay outside the terms of reference of the Expenditure Committee. An Early Day Motion was placed on the Order Paper for May 1973 on the question whether the Trade and Industry sub-committee could conduct an enquiry into wages and conditions of South African workers, and on 14 May William Clark tried to get an Emergency Debate on the matter under Standing Order No. 9. The Speaker however would not permit this debate. William Rogers, the chairman of the sub-committee, and certain other sub-committee members remained keen to undertake this enquiry, and after talks with the Government it was agreed that there was just enough connection between the general theme of Public Expenditure and South African wages to allow the sub-committee to proceed—a certain amount of money allocated to support overseas trade included a small sum spent for this purpose in South Africa. The link between the subject and spending was tenuous but it was enough. In 1974 Trade and Industry conducted a relatively small enquiry into *Milk Production*, a concession to the fact that Agriculture fell within its remit. Since that date it has concentrated its efforts on large-scale enquiries into specific decisions regarding public spending on support for the *Motor Vehicle Industry* (which concerned Government spending on British Leyland) and *Public Expenditure on Chrysler UK Ltd*. The style of this sub-committee is nowadays to take subjects of immediate interest, where particular decisions have been or are being made to spend public money, and then to analyse the rationality of the decisions in the light of the full factual background of the state of the industry concerned.

The freedom of choice that sub-committees enjoy in the selection of their topics is in fact far from absolute. A major constraint, not overt in most cases, is the one imposed by the Government, for the Government may be the main, or even the only, source of information. When a sub-committee decides to tackle a relatively small scale or technical topic in which the Government Department concerned is itself interested, then that sub-committee can expect a degree of Departmental co-operation resulting in a flow of information from civil service witnesses which can be used in the Report. Some chairmen are also attracted to the small scale type of enquiry for the reason that it allows them to make very specific recommendations, even though these may be of a minor character. By monitoring the actions of a Department affected by such recommendations, a sub-committee can soon discover whether the Department has done anything to implement them. This power of monitoring gives sub-committee members the notion that they are actually achieving something, albeit of a limited nature. The notion appeals to those sub-committee chairmen and members who regard the role of the backbench M.P. as no more than marginal with respect to administration and policy making. One member of the Defence sub-committee stated in interview:

> If the Committee were to get too deep into policy making, it would lead to a fragmentation of the policy process; and if there is fragmentation of the policy process decisions do not get made. The responsibility for Defence policy decisions lies with the Executive—it is right that it should do.[3]

The opinion that sub-committees should not break through the restraints imposed by Government conforms to the 'minimalist' view of Parliament's power versus the Executive. Some sub-committees, however, take a very different attitude to Governmental constraints. One sub-committee chairman stated that 'the Committee should not just look at the Estimates, but at policy before it is made. It should be looking at difficult issues requiring political judgement.'[4]

When a sub-committee decides to take on a wide ranging enquiry involving much Departmental work and perhaps opening up questions of policy that Departments and Ministers would prefer not to see exposed, then it may find co-operation limited. It may even be warned off the subject by the Government on the grounds that it is unlikely to be able to afford co-operation. Nevertheless, chairmen have the option of tackling politically significant or broad subjects, in spite of the constraints. They may judge that it is worth doing so in order to expose the activities of Government, even if it is clear from the outset that whatever the sub-committee may say, may reveal or recommend, will have little observable effect in terms of actual changes in administrative practice or Government policy. Thus it is clear that a sub-committee, when choosing a subject, must balance its freedom of choice against the strategy which the Government will deploy against it. Some committee chairmen respond to the Government with caution; others determine to stick out their necks.

Another constraint in the choice of topic comes from the operation

[3] Interview.
[4] Interview.

of the party system in the House of Commons. As a rule sub-committee chairmen avoid topics likely to arouse party passions and create splits among the membership of their sub-committee. Dissention can be prevented by selecting small-scale technical subjects or topics concerned with the process of decision making and by avoiding specific areas of policy or specific decisions. Occasionally sub-committee chairmen have flouted this norm and selected topics likely to inflame party feelings. The most notable example has been the above-mentioned enquiry by Employment and Social Services into pay beds in the National Health Service. The subject could have been examined in a non-partisan manner, for it had largely disappeared from party dispute. The chairman however wished it to be revived as a party issue, and ensured that the enquiry developed a political flavour with resultant conflict arising between members. Other apparently political topics such as the wages of South African workers have been managed in such a way as to minimise conflict. Political topics need not necessarily divide a sub-committee strictly along party lines. Some of the subjects studied by the General sub-committee in recent years have been in the context of very different views about the management of the economy and the causes of inflation. At the end of the enquiry into *The Financing of Public Expenditure* (1975) some left-wing members were unhappy about the slant of the Report. The split was not on party lines, however, but between some members of the Labour party and the others. At the meeting of the full Committee when it deliberated on the General sub-committee's Report, a number of votes were taken including one on an alternative Report by the left-wing Labour member, Brian Sedgemore. He was, however, only supported by two other M.P.s, while the remainder of the Labour Members at the meeting sided with the Conservatives. Policy issues, when the full facts and evidence are revealed, rarely divide committee members neatly between Labour and Conservative. This is because sub-committees have to deal with the realities of a subject rather than remain dazzled by its appearance. One ex-member of the Defence sub-committee, now a Cabinet Minister, has stated 'The Select Committees should look at money. Money is the key. We should stop the artificiality of the party political battle, and M.P.s should be M.P.s, not party men.'[5] Because the Report has to be related to the facts presented, the scope for party divisions in the Expenditure Committee is limited. It is this fact which the more ideologically minded M.P.s (of both left and right persuasions) are fully aware of and which,

[5] Interview.

incidentally, ensures their opposition to the extension of the committee system in the British Parliament.

The selection of topics for enquiry also raises the old question of whether Select Committees should deal with 'policy' or with 'administration'. It is often argued that if a Select Committee undertakes issues of policy, then it is unlikely to be able to work in a non-partisan manner. Some sub-committee chairmen obviously take this view and consider that they should restrict themselves to questions of administration and of 'value for money'. As the years have passed, however, some of the sub-committees seem to have acquired more confidence in their ability to tackle questions related to policy or to the policy making process. In this respect they are moving a small way towards fulfilling some of the more optimistic expectations of their role. This growing confidence is in part the result of experience. Members have learned that it is almost impossible to draw a clear line of distinction between 'policy' and 'administration' where money is concerned. It has been easier for the Expenditure Committee to venture into policy fields than it was for the 1966 Crossman specialist committees, for its work has always been linked to the theme of public spending. Public spending is by its very nature concerned both with policy and with administration, and any attempt to draw an absolute demarcation line is fruitless. Continual linking of money and expenditure allows almost any subject to be studied from the point of view of value for money.

Once again, we should stress that discussions of policy need not lead to party strife. If we contrast the work of the Education and Arts sub-committee with the work of the Crossman Select Committee on Education (1965), we can see how the theme of value for money has led in the case of Education and Arts to a less politically charged atmosphere by providing a sense of direction not related to party differences. Education and Arts were able to study postgraduate training in a cool atmosphere because it concentrated on cost-effectiveness factors in universities which it saw (or thought it saw) as the means to certain aims. The enquiries of the Education Select Committee on the other hand were conducted in a heated atmosphere because they delved into the difficult (and non-financial) question of university authority and discipline. Because of the continual theme of money the Expenditure Committee has found that one of its best roles is to discover means of achieving political aims rather than argue from ignorance about which of the different political ends are desirable. The link with money also means that the Committee needs to concern itself with information rather than with opinion. The emphasis on information is an important factor in the development of consensus among the sub-committee group and helps to ensure the production of agreed Reports based on facts. The need to produce consensus among the sub-committee and to issue agreed Reports is in itself a constraint upon the Committee's operation. For if a sub-committee wants its labours to have any impact on the remainder of the House, on the Government, and on the public, it must appear united.

The choice of topics and the manner in which they are investigated is thus affected both by the external constraints from Government and party, and by the internal constraint imposed by the necessity of obtaining sub-committee consensus. The general effect of the various constraints is that it leads to a narrowing of the scope of enquiries and a fragmentation isolating the topics selected by one sub-committee from those selected by another.

This survey of the topics investigated by the sub-committees shows the extent to which they have confined themselves to analysis of spending on individual items of Government, on the work of individual Departments, and on particular decisions. Only rarely have their studies pertained to over-all levels of spending, to spending on particular functions, or to the decision making process. There are, of course, variations among the sub-committees, and some, notably General and Defence and External Affairs, have widened the scope of their enquiries to encompass some of the broader aspects of public spending that it was hoped the Expenditure Committee would tackle. Even these two sub-committees however still like to spend some of their time on individual, particular issues.

The autonomy of the sub-committees (within the constraints discussed above) and the consequent fragmentation of their work means that the subjects examined do not allow for inter-Departmental or inter-functional comparisons of spending. Some sub-committees have, over the years, managed to develop a degree of continuity in their work so as to produce a sequence of enquiries each related to the other.[6] The practice of sequential enquiries becomes possible if and when a sub-committee has a relatively stable membership which is interested in following up the work it has done in previous sessions. The practice

[6] The work done by the General sub-committee on the form and presentation of Expenditure White Papers, and by the Education and Arts sub-committee on Further and Higher Education, Postgraduate Training and Decision Making in the DES are examples of sequential enquiries by individual sub-committees. Much of the work of the Defence and External Affairs sub-committee is concerned with redeveloping themes explored in earlier enquiries. Trade and Industry has shown a continued interest in public expenditure on the motor industry.

allows the sub-committee to keep watch on the responses of the Department to previous recommendations and return to further enquiries on those subjects where they feel that responses from Government have been unsatisfactory. The limit on sequential enquiries is set by the very wide range of subjects which a functional sub-committee like Trade and Industry, Environment, or Employment and Social Services can possibly investigate within its terms of reference—a concentration on one aspect of its work means that a sub-committee has to ignore other aspects. But while individual committees may be able to develop a long-term outlook on the spending of specific Departments or on specific functions, the fragmentation of their work makes it impossible for the Expenditure Committee to think in terms of allocation of resources among competing functions of Government. Like debates on matters concerned with public spending on the floor of the House, the effect of the Expenditure Committee's work is to perpetuate an atomistic approach to the problems of expenditure. It has provided no mechanism for comparing the different functions of Government, or the relative priorities of spending, or the different degrees of value for money obtained in each. This may be important where one function of Government is closely related to others. If a Government spends money with the aim of alleviating poverty or removing deprivation, it allocates it for a variety of functions such as education, housing, health and social security. The sub-committees of the Expenditure Committee have not in their first six years come together to examine the effectiveness of spending aims of Government that involve a number of Departments or separate functions. The atomistic approach to public expenditure has also been found in the Cabinet, but some attempt to correct this in the social spending field (albeit a limited attempt) came with the establishment in 1975 of the Joint Approach to Social Policy (JASP), a Cabinet committee system designed precisely to deal with the conflicting demands of those Government operations that together serve broad aims and involve a number of Ministries and Departments clamouring for funds. But in contrast to JASP, the enquiries undertaken by the Expenditure Committee remain completely unrelated one to another. If the Committee were to fulfil the highest hopes held out for it at its establishment, it would have to become *generally* bolder in the selection of topics and to be less inhibited by the constraints upon it. To fulfill the expectations of those who thought that it would add a new and more rational dimension to Parliament's role in the spending process, it would still need to adopt a more integrated approach to its examination of public spending.

6 The Expenditure Committee at Work III: the Evidence

Once a sub-committee has determined the subject of its investigation, its next step is to decide what information it will require in order to write its report and make its recommendations. There are a number of ways in which it may obtain information. It may receive formal evidence, both oral and written, and also informal evidence obtained in conversations with interested persons either in the Palace of Westminster or outside. Individual members may seek information from research reports or newspapers. Finally, the Committee may obtain help from a specialist adviser, if it chooses to appoint one. Of these sources, the most important is the formal evidence submitted by witnesses. Witnesses are generally asked by a sub-committee to send in written submissions on the understanding that they may later be asked to appear in person for oral examination to elaborate on their memoranda or explain their views. The evidence so collected usually constitutes the bulk of information used by a sub-committee in making its report. It is also possible for any interested person to send in written submissions to a sub-committee on his own initiative if he so wishes, and such submissions may be published at the end of the minutes of evidence (there is no guarantee of publication). Only rarely will a person sending in written evidence without invitation be subsequently called upon to give oral evidence. Sub-committees are generally reluctant to encourage too many submissions from the general public for fear that they may be swamped with material which they have neither the time nor the staff to process. The lack of public awareness of the opportunities which the Expenditure Committee presents ensures that the sub-committees do not become overwhelmed with submissions that they have not themselves solicited.

Few members of the public are aware that much of the oral evidence of the Expenditure Committee is taken in public sessions that they may attend (Defence and Foreign Affairs is the only sub-committee that habitually takes evidence in private), even though notices of the meetings are published each week in the press, and are posted up in the Central Lobby of the Palace of Westminster. It is unusual to find members of the general public at evidence sessions of the Expenditure Committee. The public likes to see its politicians at work in the more theatrical setting of the Chamber of the House, even though it may sometimes find that after 4.00 p.m. the 'stars' who have been present in the Chamber for Question Time have left the floor to the lesser (and often duller) lights. It occurs to few of those who form the queues entering the public galleries that they might gain a deeper insight into the workings of Government if they were to watch the sub-committees of the Expenditure Committee questioning those actually engaged in the day-to-day business of spending the taxpayer's money. For there they will have the opportunity to see Government Ministers, high-level Civil Servants, representatives of local government, and interest groups, appearing as witnesses.

The Expenditure Committee has the power to send for such persons, including Government Ministers, as it thinks may contribute to its enquiries. On a mere two occasions it has been unable to compel witnesses to attend. During the 1975–76 session Trade and Industry found that it could not ensure the appearance of Mr Riccardo, head of Chrysler and a U.S. citizen. It also found itself unable to examine the Government Minister who had played a large part in the Chrysler negotiations, Mr Harold Lever. The sub-committee's request to call Mr Lever as witness was refused by the Prime Minister, Harold Wilson, on the grounds that a Select Committee of the House could only call on Ministers to give evidence on matters concerned with their Departmental duties. Mr Lever, as Chancellor of the Duchy of Lancaster, had no Departmental duties with respect to Industry and therefore, according to the Prime Minister, could not be called to answer for actions in this regard.[1] The Prime Minister's statement was a convenient excuse to prevent Mr Lever's exposure to questions of political delicacy. But it did not constitute any real threat to the general powers of the Expenditure Committee to summon witnesses.

The person chiefly responsible for selecting the witnesses is the sub-committee chairman, who together with the clerk and the specialist adviser, if one is appointed, will draw up the list of those from whom evidence is invited. Rarely do other members of a sub-committee play a major part in the choice of witnesses, although during deliberative sessions during the course of an enquiry the whole committee may confer together to suggest additional witnesses. This reflects the relatively passive attitude taken by most Expenditure Committee members to their work.[2] It is often said by committee members in defence of their passive role towards the determining of sources of information that 'the witnesses select themselves—it is clear whom we have to have'. The more narrowly based or the more technical the enquiry, the more likely is this statement to be true. Where money is spent by a single Department of the Central Government which is particularly strongly bound by conventions of secrecy, as in the case of Defence, then the only significant source of information relevant to most enquiries will be the Department and those who fulfil its functions, i.e. the Armed Services. The high level of secrecy surrounding British defence policy inhibits academics from making independent analyses of Defence spending which the sub-committee might draw upon. Where a sub-committee like General is concerned with methods of decision making covering the whole of public spending and the entire economy, the only Department with an over-all view is the Treasury, and the only other relevant witnesses are those academic and business institutions engaged in forecasting developments in the economy or

Table Seven   Witnesses Giving Oral Evidence, 1970–74

	Gen.	Def.	T&I	E&HO	E&SS	E&A	Total
Treasury Ministers	2	–	–	–	–	–	2
Central Govt. Ministers	–	1	–	4	–	–	5
Public Organisations	–	–	14	3	19	32	68
Industry and Finance	–	8	141	28	4	11	192
Academics	6	1	5	5	–	12	29
Civil Servants							
a) Treasury	10	1	8	–	1	3	23
b) Other	19	114	33	30	40	21	257
Local Authority Officials	–	–	–	80	5	24	109
Trades Unions	–	–	11	–	26	–	37
Professional Organisations	–	–	–	11	47	47	105
Interest Groups	–	–	12	8	68	14	102
M.P.s	–	1	–	–	–	–	1
Lords	1	–	–	–	–	–	1
Journalists	2	–	1	–	–	–	3
Services and Police	–	62	–	5	–	–	67

[2] See above on levels of participation, pp. 71–84.

analysing the effect of public spending on economic development. When, however, a sub-committee undertakes an investigation into an aspect of public expenditure involving other interested people who have detailed knowledge of their subject area—such as spending bodies and agencies outside the Central Government Departments including local authorities—then it needs to spread its net wide to collect such information as is required to make an adequate survey of that function of Government.

Table Seven (page 103) lists the types of information source that sub-committees rely upon.

If the various categories of information source in the Table are grouped together it will be seen that during 1970–74 there were three main suppliers of evidence: Central Government Departments and other official and semi-official bodies, including local authorities, that spend public money; interest groups; and academics, journalists and individuals. These categories may be broadly classified as the 'spending bodies', the 'clientele', and the 'independent analysts'.

Table Eight shows the extent to which each sub-committee has relied upon these three types of information source for its evidence.

Table Eight　　Oral Evidence from Major Sources, 1970–74*

	Spending bodies %	Clientele %	Independent %
Defence and Foreign Affairs	94.7	4.2	1.1
General	77.5	nil	22.5
Environment	67.8	29.4	2.8
Education and Arts	48.9	43.9	7.2†
Employment and Social Services	30.9	69.1	nil
Trade and Industry	24.4	72.9	2.7

* Percentages of total numbers of witnesses.
† Includes some academics who might be regarded in this subject area as 'clientele' rather than 'independent' witnesses.

Overall the spending bodies provide the largest amount of evidence given to the Expenditure Committee. All the sub-committees take evidence from the Central Government Departments from time to time, and some rely particularly heavily on this source. Other official spending bodies, including local government, the Armed Forces, HM dockyards, research councils, universities and hospital boards, tend to appear frequently before those sub-committees that have direct interest in their work. The 'clientele', including industry and finance, the trades unions, professional organisations, and other interest groups, appear before most sub-committees though rarely before either General or Defence. The clientele groups together contribute almost as much information to the Expenditure Committee as the spending bodies do, and in some respects it is difficult to distinguish between the interests of these two groups, for both spenders and clientele have a mutual interest in seeing that programmes and policies are defended. Often the interest groups are directly representative of those with a stake in the public sector of the economy—trade unions representing teachers, local authority employees, doctors, etc. The smallest source of evidence to the Expenditure Committee is that classified as 'independent analyst'. The smallness of this source has, as we shall see, a great impact on the work of the Committee since the pressures acting upon it are often not counterbalanced by any independent analysis or evaluation of Government programmes. For independent evaluation of public spending the sub-committees must rely upon academic and individual witnesses who have conducted research into the subjects concerned. The sub-committees have, apart from their specialist advisers, no ready access to alternative 'independent' sources of analysis. In this respect the Expenditure Committee is at a disadvantage when compared with the new Budget Committees of the U.S. Congress (established 1974). For these Budget Committees, 'independent' analysis of Government plans carried out by staff and agencies under their own control is an even more important source of information than the Government 'spenders' and the 'clientele' groups.[3]

As sub-committees vary in their reliance on different types of evidence, it is worth looking closely at the sources used by each and at the methods of selecting witnesses which each has adopted. The sub-committee relying most heavily on official sources is Defence and Foreign Affairs. This sub-committee starts with a well-defined subject

[3] The Budget Committees of the U.S. Congress draw their independent information and analysis from a number of agencies under Congressional control. These include the Committees' own staffs, the Congressional Research Service of the Library of Congress, the General Accounting Office, the Congressional Budget Office, and the Office of Technology Assessment. There are also many private sources of independent budget analysis, notably the Brookings Institution and the American Enterprise Institute.

area and consequently would be expected to have a correspondingly narrow range of information sources. Its range of source is, however, particularly narrow. Most of the evidence supplied to this sub-committee comes from the Foreign Office, from the Ministry of Defence, and from the Armed Services. These are all 'spenders'. In comparison with the use of committees in the United States by the 'military-industrial complex' to promote its interest and schemes, it is perhaps surprising that the British Defence sub-committee has not come under the influence of information from contractors. But then it, unlike its American counterparts, does not have any contracts to distribute. In one enquiry only, that into *Guided Weapons Research and Development*,[4] has the nature of the subject studied meant that the sub-committee has had to go beyond its usual sources to collect technical information. In this case it took evidence from a number of industrial firms engaged in producing guided weapons. While it may not have been captured by the 'clientele' groups demanding spending and advocating their interests, there can be no doubt that the sub-committee has been dominated by the 'spending' interests of the Departments and the services. It is not a forum for the presentation and evaluation of differing views about the levels and allocations of Defence spending. Its ability to stand back is further weakened by the curious lack of independent analysis of Defence spending in Britain. Such analysis is inhibited by the excessive secrecy surrounding Defence policy-making and by a general lack of interest in the subject. The major institution concerned with Defence studies is the Institute for Strategic Studies, whose director, Brigadier Kenneth Hunt, has served the sub-committee as specialist adviser since 1970. Only once has the sub-committee looked further to find academic analysis of Defence spending. During its enquiry in the 1974–75 session into the Defence Review Proposals it heard, for the first time, evidence from an outside expert, Mr David Greenwood, a Senior Lecturer in Political Economy (Higher Defence Studies) at Aberdeen University. The meeting on 21 January 1975, when Mr Greenwood attended, was, according to the sub-committee chairman, 'practically the first time we have met in public'. The chairman noted the lack of interest from the public: 'We did announce to the Press that this would be so (i.e. that the meeting would be held in public) but so far there are no public here'.[5]

Apart from this rare occasion when an outside analyst was called in the analysis of Defence spending has been presented to the Defence

[4] H.C. 305 of 1975–76
[5] *The Defence Review Proposals*, H.C. 259, 1974–75, p. 9.

and External Affairs sub-committee only by its specialist adviser and by the Ministry of Defence. The sub-committee has, however, also had the services of two members of the staff of the Comptroller and Auditor General's office attached to it, and Committee Members have found their assistance of great use when assessing expenditure proposals. A further source of information has been the various informal talks with workers, service men and officers that the sub-committee has held during its travels abroad to Ministry of Defence installations. As one sub-committee member has said of such sources: 'When we actually visited the forces, more information tended to come out, especially after dinner. You learn a lot that way.' But even these informal sources do not make up for the lack of independent analysis. So far the Defence sub-committee has not found a source, like the Cambridge School of Applied Economics which provides the General sub-committee with so much analysis, to produce an 'alternative' view either of overall levels of spending or of spending on different sub-functions or particular items.

Like Defence, the General sub-committee has taken a great deal of its evidence from official, mainly Treasury, sources. Apart from its larger enquiries undertaken since 1974, the General sub-committee in its studies of Expenditure White Papers and the processes of decision-making has relied almost exclusively on two sources of information, the Treasury and the Department of Applied Economics at Cambridge. Although only one person, Wynne Godley or Terry Ward, has been the designated and paid specialist adviser at any one time, teams of workers have contributed to the analysis of the economy produced by the Cambridge department as background papers and memoranda. In its links with Cambridge the sub-committee has acquired a staff of sorts through the back door and has access in depth to at least one, if only one, alternative view of public spending estimation and control. For all of its general enquiries into White Papers, Treasury methods and spending cuts these two sources of information have been paramount. The relationship between the Cambridge 'independent' view and the Treasury view happens to be particularly interesting because Mr Godley has been described as 'gamekeeper turned poacher' —he was once a civil servant in the Treasury and then later a Cambridge don and outside critic. An understanding of how Government works from inside experience is helpful to the development of an independent view (see above for the role of the members of the Comptroller and Auditor General's office in assisting the Defence sub-committee), for under a system of Government which is not particularly open outsiders can only speak from limited knowledge of the administrative system. One danger resulting from the use of outside bodies as independent critics is that they may go beyond their role as suppliers of information and conduct a dialogue with a Government Department over the heads of the committee members. Certainly some of the material produced by the Cambridge Department of Applied Economics is of such sophistication and complexity that it is clearly aimed not at the General sub-committee but at the Treasury.

In its large enquiries into broad topics the General sub-committee has had to cast its net wide in search of information. For *Public Expenditure, Inflation and the Balance of Payments*[6] evidence was collected from no fewer than five different academic sources and from the Bank of England. The sub-committee did not go to the Cambridge department this time for a specialist adviser but instead appointed Professor A. A. Walters of the London School of Economics. Mr Wynne Godley of Cambridge was a witness. Members of the committee were surprised to find that of the protagonists in the economic dispute on the causes and cures of inflation some had never met to exchange ideas and theories. Indeed so conflicting was the academic evidence that the sub-committee in its report recommended that the economists should arrange seminars to get to know one another and reach some degree of agreement. The second enquiry which has involved the sub-committee in a search for information beyond the Treasury/Cambridge confines is the one into the post-Fulton civil service. The nature of this subject ensured that a wide variety of witnesses had to be called. These included civil servants from the Secretary to the Cabinet (Sir John Hunt) downwards, ex-Prime Ministers Edward Heath and Harold Wilson, the Central Policy Review Staff, the civil service unions and academics.[7]

Apart from the special cases where the subject matter has forced the sub-committee to search widely for information, the range of sources it has utilised is small. In spite of its recognition in 1974 of the differences of opinion among economists about forecasting and about the causes and cures of inflation, it still has not pressed further and more sharply in its search for different analytical approaches to the general problems of public spending control and management. It is still very limited in the range of views it solicits. It makes little use, for example, of the numerous different commercial and academic forecasts of movements in the economy each of which provides different

[6] H.C. 328 of 1974.
[7] *The Civil Service*, H.C. 535–1 of 1976–77.

assumptions on which public spending plans may be based. It does not have the capability itself to set in motion alternative forecasts to those of the Government, although now that there is public access to the Treasury model this can be done. It would need a proper staff of its own—not just a staff coincidentally provided at Cambridge—in order for it to take upon itself independent analyses to set against those carried out by the Treasury. In 1977, recognising the need for staff assistance, it paid a visit to Washington to observe the new United States Budget process. The sub-committee held talks (not official evidence sessions) with staff in both the Executive Branch where the President's budget is produced and the Congressional Budget Office which serves, among other bodies, to provide Congress with alternative views on budgetary matters. The sub-committee cannot have failed to notice, even though its visit was a short one, that one thing is abundantly provided to support Congressional oversight of the Budget, namely, access to a variety of independent analyses of the Government's spending plans and of forecasts of changes in the economy on which these plans are predicated. Unless the General sub-committee itself gets some capacity of its own for analysis, it cannot fully develop its potential as critics of the Government's overall spending strategy. It has taken upon itself this role, as we can see from the topics it has studied, but without playing it to the full. The point is that General, unlike Defence which deals with areas of secret planning, meets relatively few institutional barriers restricting its search for information. There is still overmuch secrecy surrounding the Chancellor's budget statement but this is only one of the means by which information about spending is revealed to the House of Commons. The Treasury model of the economy is available to M.P.s, and there is an abundant available supply of alternative views of the economy from the universities (besides Cambridge), business schools and city firms.

While Defence and, to a lesser extent, General are necessarily orientated towards collection of information from official bodies, the other four sub-committees must, owing to the nature of their subjects, collect theirs from a wider variety of source. The extent to which they are dependent on information from 'spenders', 'clientele', and 'independents', varies both from sub-committee to sub-committee and from enquiry to enquiry. As Table Eight (page 104) shows, Environment takes well over, and Education and Arts nearly, 50 per cent of evidence from spending bodies, while Employment and Social Services and Trade and Industry, take well under 50 per cent of their evidence from the same group.

Education and Arts and the Environment sub-committees take nearly equal percentages of their information from official and from non-official witnesses. The functions that these two sub-committees oversee are rather similar in so far as they are those in which local authorities and other non-Central Government agencies are large spenders. The two sub-committees also have rather similar 'clienteles'. In the case of Education and Arts most money (apart from the university sector) is spent by local authorities. Much of the money spent under the general term 'Environment' (apart from motorway and railway expenditure) is dispensed by local authorities and other semi-official agencies. These bodies are in a curious position with respect to public expenditure for they are both spenders of public money and in some sense consumers or clientele dependent upon the Central Government for a large percentage of their income. To this extent the amount of evidence collected by these two sub-committees from 'spending bodies' (see Table Eight above) may be overstated, for most spending bodies appearing before them are interested in putting forward demands for money or for particular policies to the Central Government and thus could often be regarded as 'clientele'. The local authorities, the public service unions and the local authorities' associations, being both spenders and receivers of money, soon became aware of the existence of the Expenditure Committee as a forum for the expression of their views and have as a consequence appeared time and again to give evidence. Local authority associations and teachers' unions, for example, rarely let an enquiry by the Education and Arts sub-committee go past without offering a contribution. Some of those giving evidence to Education and Arts can also be found providing information to the Environment sub-committee. The Association of County Councils and the Association of Municipal Authorities, for example, regularly submit material to both.[8]

The Education and Arts sub-committee and the Environment sub-committee basically seek two types of information from those whom they call as witnesses. They seek to know, firstly, how a particular function, programme or policy is operated by those bodies that actually spend money. How do Central Government Departments, for example, plan spending and control those who spend? In the case of

[8] See for example *Charity Commissioners and their Accountability*, H.C. 495 of 1974–75, *Education Maintenance Allowances in the 16–18 Years Age Group*, H.C. 306 of 1974 and *Priorities and Decision Making in the D.E.S.*, H.C. 621 of 1975–76 (all Education and Arts), and *Urban Transport Planning*, H.C. 57 of 1972–73, *New Towns*, H.C. 305 of 1974, and *Redevelopment of the London Dockland*, H.C. 348 of 1974–75 (all Environment).

the enquiry into *Policy Making in the D.E.S.*[9] by Education and Arts, Members were concerned to discover the methods used by the D.E.S. for setting priorities and policies. Here an important witness was the then Permanent Secretary, Sir William Pile, who in three separate oral evidence sessions explained the process in great detail. The sub-committee was also interested in the relationship between the Government Department on the one hand and those responsible for day-to-day administration, provision of services and expenditure, resultant upon these policies on the other. It therefore sought information from local authority and from teachers' representatives. Many of these groups were already familiar performers before the sub-committee, including the Committee of Vice-Chancellors and Principals, the Committee of Directors of Polytechnics, the AUT, the NUT, the NASUWT and the Association of Metropolitan Authorities. The general view expressed by these witnesses was that they, as dispensers of services, were insufficiently consulted by the D.E.S. on major policy issues. The enquiry became in fact a sort of bridge-building exercise between the Government responsible for planning and those putting its plans into operation.

Other examples of searches for factual information included the Environment sub-committee's enquiries into *House Improvement Grants*, *New Towns* and *National Parks and the Countryside*.[10] In the last mentioned enquiry it decided to examine the operation of the Countryside Act, 1968, the National Parks and Access to the Countryside Act, 1969, the effect of local government reorganisation and the future development of policy on National Parks. One thing the report revealed was the large number of public and statutory bodies with responsibility for one aspect or another of policy in the countryside, and it suggested there was need for streamlining this machinery. It said very little, however, about expenditure except to recommend that present levels of expenditure on National Parks should be maintained.

Besides concerning themselves with how Government money is actually spent, the two sub-committees have also shown interest in opinion on how such money should be spent. Environment's enquiry into *Redevelopment of the London Dockland*[11] is a good instance of this. The sub-committee sought the opinions of many bodies including local authorities and action groups to find out how people living and work-

[9] H.C. 621 of 1975–76.
[10] *House Improvement Grants*, H.C. 349 of 1972–73; *New Towns*, H.C. 616 of 1974–75; *National Parks and the Countryside*, H.C. 433 of 1975–76.
[11] H.C. 348 of 1974–75.

ing in the area thought the decline of the dockland could be halted, there being no policy in operation at the time. It found conflict between the attitudes of the councils and the Joint Committee for the Dockland (composed of local authority nominees) on the one hand and of the action groups that had arisen spontaneously in the area (such as the Joint Docklands Action Group, the Surrey Docks Action Group and the East End Dockland Action Group) on the other. These action groups had come to have a low opinion of the official Joint Docklands Committee, partly because it had no funds to do anything concrete and partly because it seemed to them to be out of touch with the views of local people. At the end of their session Mr Connolly, one of the Joint Docklands Action Group witnesses, commented, 'In thanking you (the sub-committee), could I say that, in fact, more consultation has taken place between our two sides in the last hour or so than has taken place in the last three or four years on Docklands.'[12] The sub-committee chairman, by this time somewhat bemused by the conflicting evidence he had received, replied, 'Whether it will serve your purpose any better remains to be seen.' Faced with a mass of conflicting information and opinion, the sub-committee was cautious, perhaps too cautious, in its recommendations. It proposed that the Department of the Environment should give firm guidance on the amount of public expenditure available for redevelopment. But it did not set any target figure or support any particular plan.

Both sub-committees have used the services of specialist advisers for the majority, though not all, of their enquiries. Education and Arts appointed Professor Gareth Williams from Lancaster University in 1973–74 (under its first chairman) for *Postgraduate Education* and in 1975–76 (under its second chairman) for *Policy Making in the D.E.S.* For this second enquiry it also appointed Professor Kogan of Brunel University as an adviser. Environment has often called upon the assistance of David Starkie of Reading University.[13] For its enquiry into *New Towns* it chose R. G. O. Dixon of Reading University and Murray Stewart of the University of Kent. The ways in which the sub-committee have made use of their specialist advisers have varied. In some cases the adviser has provided papers published with the Minutes of Evidence, in the same way that the Department of

---

[12] H.C. 348 of 1974–75, p. 234.
[13] For enquiries into *Urban Transport Planning*, H.C. 57 of 1972–73, *Public Expenditure on Transport*, H.C. 269 of 1974, and *Redevelopment of the London Dockland*, H.C. 348 of 1974–75.

Applied Economics at Cambridge has supplied papers for the General sub-committee. His role here has been to produce independent analysis of the function under scrutiny. Much of his other work, however, has been similar to that of the specialist adviser to Defence, namely, to provide advice and assistance in understanding and sifting information supplied by the witnesses called to give evidence.

Quite a different policy regarding advisers has been adopted since its formation by Social Services and Employment, for this sub-committee has generally worked without any specialist adviser whatsoever.[14] Social Services obtains a certain amount of its information from official sources, but it has on the whole relied more on interest groups than on either official or independent analysis. Its tendency to pay particular attention to interest groups stems in part from the topics it elects to study. These are often political in nature. Its very first topic, an overtly political enquiry into *National Health Facilities for Private Patients*,[15] drew evidence from a number of individual doctors and consultants as well as from the corporate bodies representing their interests. Much of the evidence given by individuals came as a direct result of the publicity provided in newspapers about the enquiry. Utilisation of evidence from interest groups is also marked in certain enquiries which have taken the form of a 'dialogue' between a Central Government Department and those administering and delivering the Department's services. Like Education and Arts, and Environment, the Social Services sub-committee oversees some functions of Government that are largely administered and delivered by non-Central Government Departments. As part of its remit, for example, it looks at public expenditure on the National Health Service which is operated by bodies only loosely connected with the Department of Health—indeed the weaknesses of the connections have been revealed in some of the 'dialogue' enquiry findings. The sub-committee has paid less attention to those aspects of the Social Services such as social security and national insurance that are administered centrally than it has to Health (half of its enquiries have been on aspects of the NHS) and to Employment (which is now 'hived off' into a semi-independent agency of Government).

The enquiries into *Police Recruitment and Wastage* and *DHSS Statistics*[16] are clear examples of the dialogue form. In the first case a pay

[14] Until in 1977 Rudolf Klein assisted Social Services in a short study of the relevant aspects of the Public Expenditure White Paper.
[15] H.C. 172 of 1971–72.
[16] H.C. 310 of 1974 and H.C. 312 of 1975–76.

settlement for the police was pending and the committee did a quick study of the arguments being used in the negotiations between the Home Office and the police. In the second case the junior hospital doctors had made a pay claim and were in dispute with the Department of Health and Social Security over how many doctors were being employed and how many hours they were working. An independent survey conducted on behalf of the doctors had revealed more doctors working for longer hours than the Department's figures showed. The enquiry established that the DHSS did not know how many junior doctors were employed at any given time nor how many hours they were working. Part of the trouble was the lack of co-ordination between on the one hand the Department and on the other the Area and Regional Health Authorities which were slow in passing on figures to the Department. The report also said that the communication channels between the DHSS and the doctors were sometimes 'inflexible and lacking cordiality'. In its observations on the report the DHSS replied to this particular criticism by saying that 'this is what you can expect in the middle of industrial action'.[17]

Only occasionally has the Social Services sub-committee tied its enquiries closely to public expenditure on the functions it examines. Its most recent large enquiry into *Preventive Medicine*[18] was certainly a move away from the political studies it had earlier engaged in towards a more analytical appraisal of the health services. It collected a broad range of evidence from medical experts on a variety of subjects from fluoridation of water to family planning. Some of the evidence was technical, from specialists in diseases for example, and some was from bodies with an interest to protect such as the Scotch Whisky Association. The wide range of subjects however was not well tied into the question of expenditure on the health services in general —a specialist adviser might have been of assistance here, for although the report gave details of expenditure on individual items such as alcoholism, these were not related to other expenses of the NHS. Although the sub-committee has spent so much time and effort on the NHS, it has never undertaken, until 1977 (with the help finally of a specialist adviser), an examination of the total NHS budget. In view of the constant publicity about the financial problems of the NHS and the apparently worsening relative position of Britain in the world league tables of infant mortality and other medical statistics, it

[17] *7th Special Report from the Expenditure Committee*, H.C. 571 of 1975–76 (Government Observations).
[18] H.C. 169 of 1976–77.

does seem that this sub-committee has missed a great opportunity to provide a critical examination of the way in which public money is spent on health in Britain.

Of all the sub-committees Trade and Industry has relied most on information from 'clientele' or interest groups. It has, however, frequently sought out independent analyses, where these have been available, and has been well served by specialist advisers, such as Garel Rhys of University College, Cardiff, who have prepared for it many long, analytical papers on the economics of the motor vehicle industry. It early recognised the value of independent analysis in its enquiry into *Regional Development Incentives*[19] when it discovered that academics could provide it with facts already researched on the economic effects of various regional policies. Like the General sub-committee, Trade and Industry has sometimes been able to draw upon a staff greater than is apparent from the small number of those serving as official advisers and has also been able to use witnesses as a sort of staff—as for example when it asked members of the Cambridge Department of Applied Economics to prepare a paper for the Regional Development Incentives enquiry. The volume of written memoranda produced for each of this sub-committee's enquiries has been large, but then this sub-committee has eschewed small-scale technical or political enquiries and has undertaken only six studies in as many years, most of which have been very long and have involved a great number of witnesses giving evidence. Because the subject matter (especially in *Regional Development Incentives* and in *The Motor Vehicle Industry*[20]) has been concerned with the economic effects of public expenditure, it has required factual and statistical analysis. Therefore some of the written memoranda, especially from academics, have been of considerable length and complexity. Witnesses on these occasions have not been cramped by the convention that submissions presented to Select Committees should be short.

In its enquiry into *Wages and Conditions of African Workers*[21] the sub-committee was looking for factual information as to the state of affairs and collected material from a wide range of sources. The enquiry bears some resemblance to nineteenth-century Select Committee enquiries which surveyed the state of affairs with respect to a particular issue needing regulation or Government action. The sub-committee went about the collection of information in a systematic way. All firms hav-

[19] H.C. 85 of 1973–74.
[20] H.C. 617 (188) of 1974–75.
[21] H.C. 116 of 1973–74.

ing subsidiaries in South Africa were listed and then a selection of these—the most important in terms of size—was made from which witnesses were called to provide oral evidence. There was a deliberate policy on the part of the sub-committee to ensure that the 'captains of industry' were called before it. In practice the groups of witnesses from firms were, in almost all cases, headed by the chairman of the Board and the chief directors. In selecting a representative sample of firms to give evidence care was taken to get a balance of the different degrees of control exercised by the firms over their subsidiaries or associated companies in South Africa. The last four companies called to give oral evidence were apparently summoned because they had failed to provide the sub-committee with adequate written information. Thus the sub-committee demonstrated and exercised its powers to call for 'persons and papers'.

Trade and Industry exercised equal care in the selection of witnesses for its small enquiry into *Milk Production*.[22] Both sides of the farming equation, the Ministry and the farmers, formed the major sources of information, with the dairying trade and the large dairies also giving evidence. The care with which the sub-committee approaches the selection of witnesses was demonstrated by the fact that they sought information not only from the corporate witnesses but also from those close to the actual process of milk production. They thought 'it important to invite to our committee rank and file members from the NFU and preferably from another part of the Country'. Two witnesses from near Huddersfield, one with a small and the other with a medium sized dairy farm, were called to give evidence so that the sub-committee could obtain the opinions of such farmers direct. The desire to draw evidence from production workers direct as well as from corporate bodies is also a characteristic of the sub-committee's studies of public spending in the motor vehicle industry. Beside collecting formal evidence from representatives of workers and management, members have visited factories in Britain and abroad and during these visits obtained informal evidence from those working on the shop floor. In this respect they work rather like the Defence sub-committee whose members find informal discussions during their visits away from Westminster often very illuminating. So while Trade and Industry does rely to a very large extent on the information it gathers from 'clientele' and from what are generally regarded as interest groups, it is clear that it has been well organised and careful about its approach to the

[22] *Milk Production*, H.C. 311, 1974.

collection of information. It has not assumed too blithely that it only needs to hear evidence from the representatives of the various groups in society but has accepted the fact that it may need to make its own primary investigation from time to time.

Trade and Industry's interest in analysis has been displayed from the start of its existence. In the report on *Regional Development Incentives* the sub-committee reminded the Government that public expenditure decisions require analysis of options and that the basis for political choice in that particular policy area needed improvement. 'We are far from satisfied', it said, 'that the continuing search for a viable regional policy has been backed by a critical economic apparatus capable of analysing results and proposing alternative courses' (p.72). It drew attention to the need for more efficient quantification of costs and benefits in order to provide a better basis for 'ministerial wisdom and departmental experience and judgement', for its own researches had revealed that 'regional policy has been empiricism run mad, a game of hit and miss, played with more enthusiasm than success'. The sub-committee itself has tried hard to be as analytical as possible in its approach to public expenditure, and with the exception of the *South African Wages* enquiry has concerned itself with the analysis of Government decision making and its effects on expenditure. It is obviously hampered in the extent to which it can do this by the constraints on Members' time and by the lack of its own independent analytical staff. It has however made good use of independent information from academic studies, where available, to provide it with a background of facts and figures against which the opinions of those interested parties called as oral witnesses can be set. The model of careful selection of witnesses and the backing of opinion by analysis is one which has proved successful for Trade and Industry and should be looked at more closely by the other 'subject' sub-committees.

Several obvious problems are associated with the Expenditure Committee's methods of gathering information. In the first place the general method of collecting evidence through summoning individuals or groups of witnesses is not necessarily the most sensible way to inform M.P.s about matters of Government expenditure. The Committee follows the time-honoured conventions of the House of Commons in its mode of collecting evidence, although it has extended the scope a little. The traditional methods generally result in incomplete surveys of the relevant material, and the quality and nature of the evidence (being both fact and opinion together) varies considerably. They give little scope for regular analysis of statistical information, for which in any case the Committee has not the staff resources. The Expenditure Committee follows the conventional methods partly because it is conventional in its choice of topics, and the topics, as we have seen, to a large extent dictate the sort of evidence required. It is curious that few Members have been enthusiastic about structuring their enquiries around the annual Expenditure White Papers (but then few M.P.s are particularly enthusiastic about debating the White Papers either[23]). Had they followed this route rather than selecting idiosyncratic and unrelated individual topics to study 'in depth', they would soon have run up against the fact that they could only engage in a really critical discussion of Public Expenditure with the aid of analysis of the figures contained in these White Papers and that such analysis would have to be provided either by outside advisers or through an internal House of Commons analytical staff. Some indication that a few Expenditure Committee members are aware of this problem comes in the recommendation of the General sub-committee that the Select Committees of the House should be reorganised so as to conform to the Government Departments and that they should, with the assistance of adequate specialist support staff, be responsible for consideration of appropriations of expenditure in detail.[24]

The effect of opinion and fact mixed together in the Minutes of Evidence from the Expenditure Committee needs further comment at this stage. Facts about the operation of programmes and opinion regarding policies are jumbled up together in the Minutes because the evidence is merely printed in the time order in which it was given to the sub-committee. Some sub-committees have made an effort to gather their material in a logical order, but all the effort in the world cannot produce a coherent document out of what are, after all, working papers. The printed Minutes cannot flow in an observable logical sequence as would a specially written report for a Government Department or an academic paper. Even if an M.P. wanted to read through the evidence appended to a report, he would need to take pencil and paper to make his own notes to draw together the threads of interest and argument displayed therein and to judge for himself how far the Committee's recommendations related to that evidence. The Expenditure Committee's reports con-

[23] See Chapter Two above, p. 27.

[24] *The Civil Service*, H.C. 535–1 of 1976–77 (evidence taken in sessions 1975–76 and 1976–77).

taining large amounts of undigested and unrelated information might be more useful to M.P.s if they had their own research assistants to sift through the reports for relevant material, but few have such help. Thus most reports gather dust on the shelves.

Another problem with the reports as sources of information to M.P.s not on the Expenditure Committee is that the sheer weight of material is inhibiting. 'Never read those things', said one M.P. on entering a room where Expenditure Committee reports were scattered about on chairs and tables: 'look at the size of them!' This response to a hefty 800 or 900 page report is typical. Others outside Parliament are further inhibited from using the Expenditure Committee reports as sources of information because a full set of report and evidence may cost as much as £20—a high price to pay for mere working documents rather than a coherent and structured collection of relevant data. Perhaps the time has come when the tradition of publishing all oral and solicited written evidence needs revising, for really much of the evidence is no more than general background to the report.

The other major problems consequent upon the Expenditure Committee's reliance on traditional methods of working concern the quality of the information it extracts from its witnesses. There is great variety in the size and quality of written memoranda. There is variety too in the methods of questioning witnesses in oral sessions. Some sub-committees seem more aware than others of the need to structure questioning and to relate it specifically to the written memoranda. This is perhaps easier where the memoranda give specific facts on which to hinge the questioning. The Defence sub-committee, for example, commonly prepares a line of questioning from the written evidence presented. In the enquiry into *Guided Weapons*, the chairman, addressing the managing director of the British Aircraft Corporation, explained his method: 'We have cut up your paper into eight sections. We believe that this is the easiest way to obtain your views, and it stops us asking questions in a haphazard fashion.' As a result of this structured approach to the questioning members constantly referred back to the papers submitted. Examples are: 'I notice from the paper', 'There is a reference in Appendix 3', and 'You do not say much in your paper about your relationships with the contractors' (all examples from *Guided Weapons*). Such structuring of the oral evidence sessions is not always apparent in other sub-committees, alas, and the result of failure to structure the questioning has occasionally resulted in a witness dominating the proceedings. An exceptional example of this came when Lord Fulton gave evidence to the General sub-committee during its enquiry into *The Civil Service*. After Lord Fulton had left the room and the next witness had appeared, one committee member (Nicholas Ridley) commented: 'We have not got very long, and we were unable to ask any questions at all of the last witness because he talked the whole time.'[25] More frequently witnesses prove slippery rather than dominant. Mr Joel Barnett's evidence to the General sub-committee was so full of evasive and non-committal answers that he finally provoked Nigel Lawson into saying: 'Would you try to answer the question, which is a serious one.'[26] The situation where witnesses take neither the questions nor the enquiry as a whole seriously enough occurs from time to time. During its examination of *The Motor Vehicle Industry* the Trade and Industry sub-committee noted with disfavour the attitude of certain uncooperative witnesses. Here is a section of its report:

> We feel it is a matter for profound regret that this spirit of helpful co-operation was not shown by every witness. Some of the evidence given to us by national officials of the Amalgamated Union of Engineering Workers was not satisfactory. Nor did we find acceptable the way in which Mr. Reg Birch, an Executive Councilman of the Union, gave evidence before this Committee— a Select Committee of the House. We were later informed by Mr. Scanlon, the President, and at the time, temporarily General Secretary of the Union, that the evidence in question had the full support of the AUEW Executive Council. We have made use of the evidence accordingly. Our usual practice is to summon the chairman, president or chief executive of an organisation, accompanied by such of his colleagues as he feels appropriate. On this occasion, we had excused Mr. Scanlon himself from attending as principal witness, on the grounds of the representations he made to us of the pressure of his other commitments. This is something we will be reluctant to permit in future.[27]

In spite of the deficiencies inherent in the traditional method of collecting information, we must recognise that the Expenditure Committee has increased the amount of information available to M.P.s, if they wish to make use of it, regarding the inner workings of Government. Material presented by Government Departments and other official bodies is often useful in allowing those who do take

[25] H.C. 368 xiii of 1975–76, p. 470.
[26] *The White Paper, 'Public Expenditure to 1979–80'*, H.C. 229 of 1975–76, p. 66, p. 298.
[27] H.C. 617 of 1974–75, p. 3.

the trouble to read the Minutes of Evidence to gather something they would otherwise be unable to discover about the way in which Government works. The Expenditure Committee is often better in this respect than Question Time, for it enables civil servants, as well as Ministers, to be questioned in depth. Much of what is now known about how the Treasury works with respect to the control of public expenditure has been revealed through the cross examination of Treasury and Ministerial witnesses before the General sub-committee. Similarly much useful material about the working of the Department of Education and Science has been made public through the probes of Education and Arts—though in this case the sub-committee has not learnt as much as it would like for it has found that even a Select Committee of the House can suffer from the effects of official secrecy. Official secrecy exercised by a Government Department is often a serious barrier to the effective collection of evidence by a sub-committee.

Departments often hide behind a cloak of secrecy when facing Parliament. This is as important a constraint on the operation of the Expenditure Committee as any defects in the Committee's own structure, methods, or behaviour. Information can be denied in two ways. Firstly, the Government may instruct Department officials that certain documents shall not be made available to the Committee. The Defence sub-committee has unusually good access to documentary material, for it is briefed with classified documents—if it were not, then there would be little point in its existence. But other sub-committees sometimes find limited Departmental cooperation with respect to the provision of documents. In the enquiry by Education and Arts into *Policy Making in the D.E.S.* this whole problem came out into the open when the sub-committee was refused access to Departmental planning documents—the so-called 'Policy Analysis and Review' (PAR) papers. Not long after the appearance of its report criticising the Government's excessive secrecy in refusing access to these documents, the Prime Minister (James Callaghan) announced that in the interest of more 'open' Government certain PARs would in future be made available. In August 1977 the Prime Minister also announced that after decisions had been made by the Government and revealed to Parliament then the options which had been considered in reaching the decision would also be made public. But—and this must surely be clear to everybody— unless the Expenditure Committee is able to examine these options *before* final decisions are made, it is unlikely to have any except the most marginal effect upon the course of public expenditure planning.

The second way in which the Government may hide behind the cloak of secrecy comes in the manner in which the civil servants present themselves to the Committee. They present themselves merely as spokesmen for the administration of their Departments. While they are prepared to describe the operation of a public expenditure planning process, they will not allow the Committee information about the various policy options with respect to particular decisions considered by the Department during the course of that process. Civil service witnesses usually say, when pressed on matters of what they regard as 'policy', that this is not a matter for them to answer but for the Minister. There has however been a natural reluctance on the Expenditure Committee's part to call too many Ministers before it. Since Ministers are briefed by civil servants, sub-committees have generally felt that they can obtain the information more directly by calling the civil servants. Only where sub-committees are interested in the particular political judgements made on the basis of information provided by the civil service are they likely to find it necessary to call upon Ministers—for example, the General sub-committee has called upon Treasury Ministers to explain how they make judgements about public expenditure levels in the light of the information regarding the state of the economy supplied by the Treasury.[28] Now if the Expenditure Committee were to consider in more depth the annual Expenditure White Papers, or if it were to concentrate more on financial analysis of overall spending plans, then it would need to call Ministers more often—because it would have to consider various policy options. But its rather timid approach to the hard questions of public expenditure has left it open to reliance on the civil service rather than on those who make the political choices.

The quality of evidence presented by other, non-central Governmental spending bodies suffers from other, quite different drawbacks. Such bodies, unlike central Government Departments, are not inhibited either by official secrecy or by civil service/Ministerial relationships from revealing all that the Expenditure Committee might like to know, but there are other limitations on the utility of the information they give. They are not generally so well briefed as civil servants, nor are they so well co-ordinated in their approach.

[28] See for example the evidence of Mr Joel Barnett, Chief Secretary to the Treasury, H.C. 299 of 1975–76.

They often make the mistake of sending excessively large delegations of witnesses to give evidence, which does not help sub-committees to obtain ordered information. The apparent lack of co-ordination and coherence in their information, however, stems not only from their own defects but from the structures they operate which have been subject to many changes in policy and many administrative re-organisations imposed by the Central Government in recent years.[29] A striking feature of the evidence provided by these bodies is its revelation of lack of co-ordination, variety of provision, and overlaps that exist in services. In nearly every case where a sub-committee has studied a decentralised function, its report has recommended that national standards be set and national supervision of services be established.

A final, and once again, different problem relates to the evidence received from 'clientele' groups. This evidence is generally presented by the leadership of a group or corporate entity. Only very rarely do 'grass roots' or 'rank and file' members of corporate bodies appear before the Expenditure Committee. Most sub-committees are perfectly happy to assume that by calling the leaders of a group they are indeed testing the opinions of that group as a corporate body. Occasionally, however, they have questioned that assumption. The Defence sub-committee, which has had little experience with clientele or corporate witnesses, commented in its report on *Guided Weapons*: 'The more general views of industry were available to us through the SBAC's (Society of British Aerospace Companies) evidence, although their team of witnesses sometimes appeared to speak as individuals rather than on behalf of the SBAC as a corporate body.'[30] As we have shown above, Trade and Industry has sometimes sought out evidence from individuals to set against the evidence it collects from the leadership of corporate bodies. As a rule however sub-committees seem happy to continue to call for evidence from the leadership of these groups on the assumption that they accurately reflect and can articulate the opinions of their general membership. They are, of course, encouraged to make this assumption owing to lack of time and facilities for independent studies of opinion.

It is however necessary to ask to what extent do those called upon to provide information from these groups to the Expenditure Committee represent the corporative view. The question is important both

[29] The local government re-organisation of 1974 and the Health Service re-organisation of the same date are examples.
[30] H.C. 597 of 1975–76, p. x.

because much of the information on which the Expenditure Committee bases its reports comes from such sources and because the Select Committee system, especially the Expenditure Committee, is becoming for interest groups an ever more important access point to Government. During the course of one enquiry by the Education and Arts sub-committee, it was possible to make a test of the assumption that the leadership of corporate bodies has an accurate view of, and has sought out, its members' opinions. For its enquiry into *Postgraduate Training* Education and Arts sought evidence from the universities, and this evidence was provided by the Committee of Vice Chancellors and Principals and by the Association of University Teachers. In order to test the extent to which the leaders of these groups were communicating solicited views from their members, a survey was conducted in two universities to find out what members of staff of the universities knew about the current enquiry. Questionnaires were sent to the non-medical staff of the University of Bath and of University College, Cardiff. This postal survey had a high response rate of 67 per cent. The questionnaire (see Appendix A) was very short and merely asked the respondent to name the subject of the current enquiry by the Education and Arts sub-committee and then indicate (a) which types of teaching he was engaged in (undergraduate, postgraduate, other), and (b) which newspapers and journals he read regularly (from a list provided). In total there were 388 usable replies to the survey arriving before the time limit expired (i.e. before the sub-committee finished its enquiry). Of these replies only nine respondents ventured to offer the subject matter of the current Expenditure Committee enquiry. Of those nine who claimed to know the answer only one, from Bath, who subsequently turned out to have been one of the AUT delegation giving evidence, actually managed to produce the correct answer. In effect no one apart from the representatives giving evidence even knew that the enquiry was under way. These results were surprising. The organisers of the survey had not expected a very high proportion of correct answers in view of the level of ignorance that they had detected during preliminary enquiry. But in view of the efforts which Select Committees had made from 1966 onwards to involve the public in their work and in view of the fact that when the survey was taken the sub-committee enquiry had already been in progress for some time and been reported in the specialist press, they did expect that some measurable proportion of the respondents would know that an enquiry into a topic of interest to them was being made. Since many of the respondents claimed to be regular readers of newspapers and of the specialist press, their ignorance could not be explained in terms of their failure to read newspapers, although the intensity of their reading was not tested. And since more than half the respondents claimed to be engaged in postgraduate research, no one could say that the enquiry was irrelevant to them.

The importance of this story is revealed by its curious sequel. After the Expenditure Committee had produced its report, the Committee of Vice Chancellors and Principals found the recommendations not at all to its taste. Accordingly the CVVP decided to conduct its own study and sent letters to all Vice Chancellors and Principals asking them to collect opinions on postgraduate training from the members of their staff. Some did canvass opinions, but again the lines of communication were not clearly drawn. In some cases only professors of departments received the request from a vice chancellor for information about postgraduate training. Professors in their turn sometimes replied without consulting their departmental colleagues or delegated the responsibility for a reply to another member of staff, without necessarily requesting him to consult others. In certain cases, no doubt, the vice chancellor's request for information found its way to the bottom of a 'pending' file. So this survey of opinion, as that conducted by the Education and Arts sub-committee, never properly canvassed the views of those engaged in the enterprise being studied. A further survey carried out for the Earth Sciences Educational Methods Group of the Geological Society by Dr M. Brooks of the Department of Geology and Oceanography of University College, Swansea, drew attention to the recommendations of the Education and Arts sub-committee emphasising the need to relate postgraduate training to the needs of industry. The Swansea survey of postgraduate students in training showed that the majority of Ph.D students think that postgraduate training should be to train teachers and researchers. This view was hardly considered by the sub-committee. In other words the premises of the sub-committee's report were not firmly rooted in the attitudes and motivations of postgraduate students themselves. Thus the sub-committee had no more tested the opinion of the consumers than it had that of the producers of the public service whose effectiveness it was considering.

The account given here of the method of collecting information for an Expenditure Committee report indicates how the variety of approach exhibited by the sub-committees is determined by the general functional area of the individual sub-committee and by the particular subjects it chooses to study. In spite of the differing approaches and methods, however, a general pattern of gathering evidence is perceptible. The Expenditure Committee is traditional in its selection of subjects and in its methods of collecting material. It has not fully broken with the pattern set by its predecessor, the Estimates Committee.[31] Most sub-committees like to engage in long 'in depth' enquiries into specific topics and miss the opportunity to get to grips with the matter of surveillance and control of expenditure through the analysis of policy options and alternatives because of their narrow focus. The specific nature of the topics ensures that the Expenditure Committee relies upon official spending bodies and the spending 'clientele' for the bulk of its information, and that it makes relatively little use of independent analysis. Independent analysis would be essential if it were to undertake studies of policy options and alternatives over the whole range of spending or in relation to particular decisions. It is further constrained in its methods of collecting information through lack of time. Service on the Committee is only a part-time occupation for most M.P.s, an occupation indeed low on the scale of their priorities. Even those who may have expertise in methods of research rarely have the time to apply this to their Expenditure Committee work. Finally, the Committee is constrained in its search for information by the lack of its own expert research and support staff who could provide it with a source of scientifically-based information independent of both the 'spenders' and the 'clientele'. Many people have recommended greater staff for Select Committees, including the Expenditure Committee itself. But as well as some independent staff of its own the Expenditure Committee needs to develop a generally more sophisticated approach to its evidence. Its present reliance on nineteenth-century methods of collecting information ill equips it to understand the intricacies of Government spending in the twentieth century. The methods of information gathering used at present by the Committee do not help it to fulfil its potential as a scrutinizer of the Government's public spending plans.

[31] For comparison, see N. Johnson, *Parliament and Administration: The Estimates Committee, 1945–65*, Allen & Unwin, London, 1966.

7 The Impact of the Expenditure Committee

Once the period of collecting evidence is over, the chairman of the sub-committee, perhaps helped by the clerk and specialist adviser, prepares a draft report. This is considered and maybe amended in deliberative sessions of the sub-committee. Sub-committees do not report direct to the House of Commons but send their reports to the whole Expenditure Committee which issues them to the House. Thus a report may be amended and voted upon both in the sub-committee and in the Expenditure Committee, though as a rule the more significant alterations are made during the sub-committee stage. Reports are usually based upon the evidence that the sub-committee has collected rather than upon the simple prejudices and political inclinations of the chairman or group of members. So long as sub-committees follow this rule, they are not likely to divide along ideological or party political lines, nor are they likely to bring any differences they may have before the full committee. Many members interviewed spoke of the need for a bi-partisan approach.

> The bi-partisan approach to Select Committees has grown up over the years.... In Select Committees as a rule you are not working toward direct and overt party political objectives—you take a subject and look at it narrowly. We agree that we are spending the money and that, if we are, then how is it best spent.... Members do approach their work on Select Committees in a bi-partisan way; they look for a way to obtain an objective report.[1]

> We were a pretty a-political committee. There was a slight danger in the fact that we were all fairly keen on Defence—but this was the secret of our harmony.... In our committee we never—or hardly ever—had votes. I prefer it that way—where we 'trade off' rather than vote—we get there by edging all the way.[2]

> The great hope for Parliament is the bringing together of different points of view. Two Labour Members on the enquiry (*Maintenance*

[1] Interview, Labour Member on Trade and Industry sub-committee.
[2] Interview, Labour Member on Defence and External Affairs sub-committee.

Allowances) wanted higher allowances but they agreed on the report. This gives hope that M.P.s are more sensible than they appear when they get to the reality of the subject. The evidence is the reality of the situation.[3]

Members who express this type of attitude to the job of collecting evidence and writing a report tend to be relatively happy with the work of the Expenditure Committee. Indeed they would not find their participation nearly so agreeable if they did not believe that a Select Committee's task was to collect evidence and produce an agreed report on the basis of that evidence. Members like the one who expressed the following tend not to remain on the Expenditure Committee for long:

> If a Select Committee of which I was a member was to do a proper assessment of a subject, we would need to get researchers that we know, well-qualified academics, and who are on the same side politically, not biased, but on the same side of the political fence as me. They are not biased in that they would not tell lies, but they would have convictions.... Successful sub-committees in my view are those with politically contentious reports. The people of Britain then know that someone has exposed something and this provides a feast day for the radical reformers who want to get gen on something like private medicine. This sort of thing is successful in influencing party policy.[4]

The general acceptance of the need for committee consensus does not mean that a chairman has never tried to produce a report unrelated to the evidence, or that individual members have never refused to accept the majority view of what the evidence implies. In cases where major disagreements have been carried forward to the whole Expenditure Committee, however, the more 'prejudiced' view never seems to have won the day. The one obvious example of a chairman attempting to produce a report unrelated to the evidence happened during the enquiry into *NHS Facilities for Private Patients*.[5] The matter was ultimately brought to a vote in the whole Committee where the chairman hoped to get overturned a number of amendments carried by her sub-committee to her original report. In this she failed. On two occasions a left-wing group in the General sub-committee has objected to its recommendations and later forced a vote in the whole Committee, both times without success. In 1975 Mr Brian Sedgemore opposed the report of the General sub-committee (of

---

[3] Interview, Conservative Member on Education and Arts sub-committee.
[4] Interview, Member (for a short time only) of the Education and Arts sub-committee.
[5] H.C. 172 of 1971–72.

which he was a member) and brought his own alternative draft report on *The Financing of Public Expenditure* to the full committee. Two other Labour members supported him. In 1977 he led a group of members to vote for a draft alternative first chapter to the report on *The Civil Service*. This chapter was defeated in the full Committee by 15 votes to 11. On this occasion he received the support of many Labour M.P.s (including some not normally considered left-wing), but the sub-committee chairman, Mr English, and Conservative M.P.s secured a majority against. During the press conference that followed the publication of the report Mr English emphasised the bi-partisan manner in which most of the recommendations had been carried, but Mr Sedgemore insisted that an important party issue was involved. Fortunately for the harmonious functioning of the Expenditure Committee, such instances of major disagreement are unusual. Most members think that if a report is to have any impact at all, it will look better if everyone on the sub-committee agrees with it. The reason why they believe this is grounded in their perception of the relative powers and influence of Select Committees.

Select Committees are not authoritive agencies of Government.[6] They are simply groups of Members of Parliament who offer it advice. The Government may take notice of what a Select Committee proffers, but it is under no obligation to follow the Committee's recommendations. Select Committees in fact have no authority and few powers.[7] They have the power to call for papers and persons, to travel outside Westminster to collect evidence (since 1968 a sum of money has been set aside in the Annual Estimates to provide for travel by Select Committees), and to appoint specialist advisers. But Select Com-

---

[6] 'The word "authority" then, denotes a formal consideration, independent of all others, in which an utterance or an action is identified, understood and responded to, not in terms of what it prescribes or of the personal qualities of an agent or the confidence he inspires, but in relation to an office, a practice or a procedure, or a rule recognised as such.' Michael Oakeshott, 'The Vocabulary of a Modern European State', *Political Studies*, vol. XXIII (June–September 1975). Nos. 2–3, pp. 321–22. According to David J. Bell, *Power, Influence and Authority*, O.U.P., New York, 1975, p. 12, those exercising authority do not bargain or plead; they order.

[7] 'The word "power" may mean merely "force" (such as that of wind or water), or it may denote the energy a man may intentionally exert to destroy, to manipulate or to overcome the resistance of an object (or of another man considered merely as an object), but in human affairs it stands for the ability to procure with certainty a wished for response in the conduct of another.' Oakeshott, *op. cit.*, pp. 321–22. This response is achieved through the use of resources. Bell, *op. cit.*, p. 12, says that power implies consequential action if a request is not complied with. The consequential action with respect to Select Committees would be a statement of the abuse of Parliamentary privilege. This is a very limited resource.

mittees like the Expenditure Committee have no overt sanctions to impose on a Government that does wish to comply with their suggestions. There is no consequential action which a Committee can take to force a Government to change its policy or methods, except that, having won the power to choose its own topics for study, a sub-committee of the Expenditure Committee can always return to a subject on which it feels the Government needs prodding. This is hardly sanction, however; more an expression of influence.

Given therefore the very limited power that the Expenditure Committee wields, we can understand why the majority of its members should be concerned with presenting a common front to the Government and/or to Departments when it issues reports. All members can realistically hope for is that the reports will have some degree of influence on the Executive.[8] Disunity in their ranks merely dissipates the chances that they will influence anybody. But there are question marks even over the degree of influence that they hold over Government. Does the work that they do have any impact at all on Government policies and administrative practices? Is the Expenditure Committee able to display to the government the consequences resultant upon particular actions, policies or decisions? And how does such influence, if it occurs, come about?

It is no easy task to trace the influence of any institutional body in the decision-making process. The task is especially difficult in the case of Select Committees whose powers are few and whose public statements rarely result in immediate changes in Government practices. Because such Committees have so little immediate effect, some commentators assume that they are a waste of time.[9] The same is felt in the particular case of the Expenditure Committee by a few of its members and ex-members.

> There has been an agitation on the part of the Committee for a greater acknowledgement by the Government for the work it has done. The reports which it produces are not being given their rightful place by the Government. The Government tends to say: 'Let us ignore it; let us put our heads in the sand'.[10]

[8] For the meaning of 'influence' see Talcott Parsons, 'On the Concept of Influence'. *Public Opinion Quarterly*, vol. XXVII (Spring 1963). David Bell, *op. cit.*, distinguishes influence from power in the sense that influence is in essence a means of persuasion which involves giving reasons or justification for doing certain things and avoiding others. Influence is backed up by arguments of the type: 'If you do X, you will feel Y', and displays the consequences which will flow from doing X.

[9] S. A. Walkland, 'The Politics of Parliamentary Reform', *Parliamentary Affairs*, XXIX, No. 2, Spring 1976, pp. 199–210.

[10] Interview, Conservative member of Education and Arts sub-committee.

But many other members of the Expenditure Committee do not see their impact in terms of immediate changes of course by the Government: 'Even if the recommendations of the committee are not accepted by the Government, they can be valuable—they force people to think about the subject and they may lead to modifications in policy.'[11]

Making others think about a political matter in a new light amounts to the exercise of a degree of political influence, however subtle and unmeasurable such influence might be.[12] When people try to measure the actual degree of influence which the Expenditure Committee has on the Government, they take the most obvious first course of looking at the effect it has not on thoughts but on specific decisions, policies, actions and processes of Government. They ask what actual changes can be seen to have taken place as a result of the Committee's work. At once problems of measurement arise, because there are two types of effect that an Expenditure Committee report can have. Firstly, it may have a recognisably short-term effect when a Department rapidly accepts specific and detailed recommendations, such as those suggesting changes in the form and presentation of Expenditure White Papers. However, even in these apparently clear-cut cases where the Department seems to agree with the recommendations, it may be difficult to estimate the exact degree of influence wielded by the Committee itself, for the Department may already be interested in effecting the changes concerned and Departmental witnesses may even have implanted ideas to that effect in the minds of the Committee members. Secondly, Committee recommendations may have a long-term effect, even if they are not immediately acted upon, provided they are in line with at least a section of Departmental thinking. In such cases they may become Departmental policy later. Sometimes the Committee may make recommendations which, while not acceptable to the current Government, will be taken up by a future Government after a change of power. The difficulty of establishing the precise influence of the Expenditure Committee in effecting long-term policy and administrative changes is that it may be only one among many bodies and individuals urging such changes upon the Government. Once a period of time has elapsed, it is difficult to see the extent to which the Committee recommendations rather than other material

[11] Interview, Conservative member of Education and Arts sub-committee.
[12] The problem of measuring power and influence and the distinction between what is overt and measurable and what is covert and non-measurable is discussed by P. Bachrach and M. S. Baratz, 'Two Faces of Power', *APSR*, vol. LVI, (1966), pp. 947–52, and by Stephen Lukes, *Power: A Radical View*, Macmillan, London, 1974.

received by the Government have influenced its decisions.

Some clearer idea of the short-term effect can be gained from an analysis of the Government's stated replies to the Committee's recommendations. It is the custom of the Government to issue, some time after the publication of an Expenditure Committee report, its own Departmental Observations. These generally appear as White Papers or are published as Special Reports of the Expenditure Committee. The amount of time that elapses between publication of a Committee report and publication of the Government's reply is often considerable. In 1976 there were complaints from Committee members that replies to some reports were two years outstanding. The more normal lapse of time is about six months. There is no urgency on the Government to produce its observations, since no special time is set aside for debates on Expenditure Committee reports on the Floor of the House. Only where a report raises a matter that is urgent or of political interest will M.P.s be concerned with wringing a response from the Government. Early in its life the Defence and External Affairs sub-committee was unhappy about the length of time between publication of its report and the appearance of the Government's observations. In the Fifth Special Report from the Expenditure Committee the sub-committee rapped the Department on the knuckles. It noted that the first set of observations had been produced 'in response to the Committee's urgent request'. These observations had been received by the sub-committee on Thursday, 20 July, and the report was due for debate in the House on Monday, 24 July, no less than five months after it had been published. The sub-committee commented: 'We consider such a delay to be quite unsatisfactory, and to imply a serious discourtesy to the House on the part of the Ministry'.[13] Relations between the Ministry of Defence and the sub-committee have improved since then, in part because the sub-committee has been vigilant in following up the course of its recommendations through the Department and because it returns to the same subjects year after year, not allowing civil servants to rest secure in the thought that it will not reopen old subjects. Further complaints about Department delays have been made subsequently by other sub-committees that do not enjoy such a close relationship with Departments. On 20 November 1972 Labour M.P.s signed an Early Day Motion stating 'that this House deplores the dilatoriness of the Secretary of State for Social Services in presenting his considered reply to the Report of the Expenditure Committee on National Health Facilities for Private

[13] *Fifth Special Report from the Expenditure Committee*, H.C. 451 of 1971–72, p. v.

Table Nine   Sample of Production of Departmental Observations

Subject	Report published	Observations published	Delay (months)
Probation & After Care	Dec. 1971	May 1972	6
Defence Expenditure	Feb. 1972	Jul. 1972	5
Private Practice in the NHS	Mar. 1972	Apr. 1973	13
Public Money in the Private Sector	Jul. 1972	Dec. 1972	5
Defence Expenditure	Oct. 1972	Feb. 1973	4
Further & Higher Education	Dec. 1972	Jul. 1973	7
Urban Transport Planning	Dec. 1972	Jul. 1973	7
Defence Expenditure (Gibraltar)	Feb. 1973	May 1973	3
Youth Employment Employment of Women } Employment Agencies	Feb. 1973	Jan. 1974	9
Visit to Washington and Ottawa	May 1973	Nov. 1973	6
House Improvement Grants	May 1973	Jan. 1974	6
Postgraduate Education	Dec. 1973	Aug. 1976	32
Regional Development Incentives	Dec. 1973	May 1975	18
Accident & Emergency Services	Jan. 1974	Jan. 1975	12
Wages & Conditions of South African Workers	Jan. 1974	Dec. 1974	11
Defence Expenditure	Feb. 1974	Apr. 1974	2
Defence Expenditure	Jul. 1974	Nov. 1974	4
Milk Production	Jul. 1974	Jan. 1975	5
Police Recruitment & Wastage	Jul. 1974	Apr. 1975	9
Educational Maintenance Allowances	Jul. 1974	May 1976	22
Public Expenditure on Transport	Jul. 1974	Mar. 1975	8
Public Expenditure, Inflation and the Balance of Payments	Jul. 1974	Jun. 1975	11
Defence Expenditure	Mar. 1975	May 1975	2
Defence Expenditure	Jul. 1975	Dec. 1975	5
The Children & Young Persons Act	Jul. 1975	Apr. 1976	9
New Towns	Aug. 1975	Sept. 1976	13
The Financing of Public Expenditure	Dec. 1975	Feb. 1976	2
The White Paper 'Public Expenditure to 1979–80'	Mar. 1976	May 1976	2
D.H.S.S. Statistics	Mar. 1976	Jul. 1976	4
National Parks & the Countryside	Jun. 1976	Mar. 1977	9
Guided Weapons	Jul. 1976	Dec. 1976	5
Policy Making in the D.E.S.	Jul. 1976	Nov. 1976	4

Patients; notes that this Report was ordered to be printed on 2nd March; and demands both the Minister's reply and an opportunity for an early debate'. They had however to wait a further five months before the Minister responded. Unfortunately Governments continue to take their time in framing their replies, as Table Nine (page 133) indicates. One excuse put forward to explain the delays is that a Department needs time to circulate memoranda and in some cases to consult other Departments. Perhaps if there were a fairly high-level co-ordinator for responses to Expenditure Committee reports, speedier action on recommendations might follow. However the Departments are not in general geared up to produce fast reactions to any outside influences upon them.

Examination of the contents of Departmental observations reveals a variety of responses, and these may be categorised under the following headings:

1. agreement to specific action;
2. agreement with the recommendations but no commitment to specific action;
3. agreement with the principle embodied in the report but no agreement to action on the grounds of high cost or of low cost-effectiveness;
4. comment that the matter is being kept under review;
5. passing the buck;
6. general statements of a non-committal nature;
7. rejection of the recommendations.

Just occasionally a Department states that the recommendations are already in line with current Government policy.

Agreement upon a commitment to specific action generally occurs on matters of detail or alternatively where a commitment to change has already been made or considered by the Department. Here are some instances of positive Departmental response. After some prodding by the Defence and External Affairs sub-committee, the Ministry of Defence agreed to present the figures for expenditure on health, married accommodation and education as separate items in the annual statement on Defence Expenditure. The same sub-committee succeeded in persuading the NAAFI to reduce some of its prices in Gibraltar. Following the recommendations of the General sub-committee, the Treasury agreed to changes in the presentation of the annual Expenditure White Papers. The Employment and Social Services sub-committee suggested that the provision of youth employment services should be mandatory upon local authorities. The Department accepted this idea and indicated in its reply the specific action that would be taken. Several of the recommendations of the report on *Private Employment Agencies* were later covered by the provisions of the Employment Agencies Act 1973. There are a number of other Committee recommendations which Departments have accepted.

Agreement but with no commitment to specific action is common where bodies outside the Central Government Departments are the spending agencies. An example of this category of response occurred in the case of *Educational Maintenance Allowances in the 16–18 Age Group.* The Secretary of State for Education claimed that the Government was in sympathy with the Committee on many of the points it had made in its report but that the Government promised no action apart from 'study of these problems in depth'. In the present circumstances, he said, 'the Government are not in a postion to contemplate any immediate action. As and when that situation changes, the Government will of course discuss with the local authorities any new proposals they may then have.'[14] In a number of cases the Department will go a little further, yet still without committing itself to action, by agreeing to 'encourage', 'advise', or 'communicate' the recommendation to the spending body. Several such responses are to be found in the observations on the Environment sub-committee's report on *Urban Transport Planning.* The Committee recommended, for example, that local authorities should be encouraged to make more widespread use of pedestrian precincts. The Department accepted this recommendation and stated that 'a bulletin of advice, to encourage the introduction of still more schemes, is to be prepared'.[15] The sending out of a bulletin may appear to constitute specific action on the part of the Department, but it does not entail action on the part of the spending body. The Committee's tendency to make vague recommendations to the effect that such an action 'should be encouraged' is itself a reason why Departments make this sort of reply. The vagueness destroys the sense of urgency which a report should generate.

Sometimes a Department will agree that an idea is a worthy one but that previous consideration has revealed either that it is very expensive or that other methods of achieving the same objective are cheaper. In response to the Defence and External Affairs' recommendation of an English Language television service for B.A.O.R.,

[14] *Sixth Special Report from the Expenditure Committee*, H.C. 428 of 1975–76.
[15] Cmnd 5366, July 1973, p. 8.

the Ministry replied that this proposal had been considered several times and rejected because 'it is one of a number of further improvements.... but there are many competing demands on the limited amount of money that is available'.[16] The same sub-committee's suggestion that a study should be made of the use of helicopters for moving troops, equipment and stores, was also rejected because of high costs. 'On cost grounds alone', so stated the Ministry, 'this idea is not being considered further',[17]

Departments often say that a matter is being 'kept under review'. This phrase means very little. It is commonly used to dismiss specific recommendations while yet trying to create the impression of Departmental concern. Instances where the phrase has been used include the Government's response to the report on *Probation and After Care*, which recommended that forecasts of manpower requirements for the probation service should be re-examined, and several responses to reports of the Defence sub-committee. The sub-committee recommended, for example, that the Ministry of Defence should conduct an enquiry into the procedure of controlling stores and into the write-off powers of commanding officers. The Ministry considered that the present powers of write-off were generally adequate, but that 'particular aspects of write-off powers, and more general ones, arise at sufficiently frequent intervals for the whole subject to be kept under review.'[18] Four years later the Department was still using this phrase in reply to the Defence sub-committee's recommendations for improving the morale of British forces in Hong Kong.[19] The significance of this is that Defence, the most vigilant sub-committee in its monitoring of Departmental reactions, should still after such a long time find it difficult to ensure meaningful responses to all its proposals.

Where much of the spending of public money is undertaken by bodies other than the Central Government Departments, the response to Expenditure Committee recommendations may take the form of 'passing the buck'. In its 1973 observations on the *Urban Transport Planning* report the Department of the Environment said that it thought it was wrong to seek detailed control of the transport decisions of local authorities. The Department of Employment's reply to the report on *Youth Employment Services* (observations published 1974) belongs to the same category. With respect to recommendations

---

[16] *Fifth Special Report from the Expenditure Committee*, H.C. 451 of 1971–72, p. vii.

[17] *Fifth Special Report*, 1971–72, p. ix.

[18] *Fifth Special Report*, 1971–72, p. viii.

[19] Government Observation on the 3rd Report from the Expenditure Committee (Hong Kong and Cyprus, H.C. 270 of 1975–76), Cmnd 6499, June 1976.

regarding careers teachers in schools, the Department stated: 'It does not however think that it would be right to depart from the principle that decisions about the employment of particular categories of teachers should be left to the LEAs and the governing bodies of secondary schools to make in the light of local circumstances'.[20] It is this sort of response which indicates that the Expenditure Committee should sometimes seek observations from other bodies spending public money as well as from Departments of Central Government.

From time to time the Departmental observations are couched in very general terms of a non-committal nature. This may occur where a Department is confronted with a suggestion to which it had not previously paid much attention. The Employment and Social Services sub-committee in its report on *The Employment of Women* recommended that officers with specialist knowledge of the matters most closely affecting women at work should be available to give advice in job centres. The Department replied in 1974 that the Government was confident that the much improved training of employment advisers being introduced would enable them to provide the standard of counselling service envisaged by the committee. Departments may also issue non-committal replies to reports which, like those referred to above in one of the other categories of response, contain vague suggestions and comments. Indeed loose phrasing in reports even allows Departments to ignore sub-committee comments altogether. The Defence sub-committee noted 'with regret' that official Government response from the Foreign and Commonwealth Office is usually restricted to specific recommendations of reports and ignores many pertinent comments, criticisms and suggestions. It therefore recommended that Departmental observations in future should include replies to all major comments—a practice that had hitherto been adhered to only by the Ministry of Defence in replies to the sub-committee.[21]

Finally, certain recommendations in reports are rejected because they conflict with Departmental practice or Government policy. Most of the recommendations by the Education and Arts sub-committee in its 1972 report on *Further and Higher Education* were later rejected by the Government which referred the committee back to the proposals made in the 1972 White Paper *Education: a Framework for Expansion* (Cmnd 5174). The Government did not agree with the committee's suggestion that the present quinquennial and rate support grant arrangements

---

[20] Government Observations on the Reports on Youth Employment Services, The Employment of Women, and Employment Services and Training, Cmnd 5536, p. 6.

[21] *Diplomatic Manpower and Property Overseas, 1976 Review*, H.C. 604 of 1976–77.

for funding further and higher education inhibited satisfactory long-term planning. It did not share the committee's view that 'the existence of two separate sectors of higher education financed from different sources is not conducive to the most efficient distribution and use of total resources available'.[22] The committee had recommended that a commission be set up to deal with the whole higher education system. The Government thought that it would be too large, cumbersome in operation and ineffective. If, as suggested, it were to have supervisory powers over education courses, it would become too much of a centralised bureaucracy and would diminish the scope of the Education Secretary's accountability to Parliament. The Government agreed with the Committee only on the matters of student accommodation and grants.

Another notable example of rejection of recommendations came in the Government's response to the Trade and Industry report on *The Motor Vehicle Industry*. While acknowledging the contribution made by the Expenditure Committee report and the value of the evidence collected, the Government shared little of the Committee's anxiety concerning the principle of granting public funds to an uneconomic industry (British Leyland). The suggestion of the Committee that the Government had already decided upon the form of action before the Ryder enquiry (the Government's own investigation into the economic viability of British Leyland) began was firmly rejected. The Committee's fears of continuous Government subsidy and possible interference in the day to day running of the company were dismissed as unfounded. British Leyland, said the Government, was in no danger of becoming a permanent 'pensioner'.

These two examples of rejection by the Government are notable in the light of subsequent events. The long-term planning of higher education, deemed unsatisfactory by the Expenditure Committee, is by 1977 in a worse state of disorder, due to the suspension of the quinquennial grant system during the period of inflation, the incomes policy, and the 1976 'cash limits' system. Subsequent to the Government's dismissal of *The Motor Vehicle Industry* recommendations, it has had to support Chrysler financially (on which decision the Trade and Industry sub-committee conducted a further enquiry) and in late 1977 pay a further £50 million through the National Enterprise Board to British Leyland, not for investment purposes but just to pay wages. Both Committee reports concerned had tried to inject an element of rational economic consideration into public spending

[22] Cmnd 5368, July 1973, p. 3.

choices. The Government however has not let the economic factors revealed by the reports form the basis of its decisions in these particular matters.

Government inaction following Expenditure Committee reports is common Government action is rare. Some criticism for this state of affairs must rest with the Committee itself. It does not help matters by choosing to study broad issues, often only indirectly related to public spending, the nature of which encourages vague recommendations and does not leave sufficient concrete points with which to prod Departments into action. The Committee cannot compel Departments to follow up its recommendations, even if these Departments express general agreement with them, but the sub-committees can help themselves more, as Defence has learned to do, by returning again and again to a Department to discover what actual action has taken place on recommendations. The continuity of membership that the Committee now enjoys should make such practices more common. A particular weakness of the Committee in its relations with the spending bodies is that it concentrates its efforts on obtaining responses from the Central Government Departments and does not seek observations on reports from other spending bodies. Since one-third of all public expenditure in Britain is spent by bodies other than Central Government, this is a serious defect. Central Government has only tenuous responsibilities for actual outlays of money on many services. So if the Expenditure Committee wishes to see its recommendations carried through, it will have to dig deeper into the Government structure to obtain responses from those who make day to day spending decisions. The fragmentation of the modern administrative structure in Britain weakens the ability of Parliamentary bodies to control the administrative process. The failure of the Expenditure Committee to obtain replies to its suggestions from bodies beyond the Central Government increases the impression that it has little impact on overall spending.

Examination of the impact of the Expenditure Committee in terms of immediate Government responses to its recommendations inevitably leads to the conclusion that it has had an extremely limited effect. In seven years it has heard over 2000 witnesses and produced over 80 reports. Of its many recommendations only a handful have been implemented. The Committee itself is not happy with the Government's attitudes towards it. In December 1975 it issued a Special Report commenting upon the effect of sluggish Departmental reaction: 'We find it disappointing that much of the effort of our Sub-committees in producing informed Reports on important and topical matters is frustrated by the failure of Government Departments to comment upon our conclusions and recommendations.'[23]

Those holding 'minimalist' expectations of the possible role for the new Committee have been proved right if its success is measured solely by Government reactions. It has not done as much to redress the balance of power between Executive and Parliament as the 'maximalists' hoped it would. But to look at the impact of the Committee merely in terms of power relationships is to ignore its capacity for more indirect influence. The direct approach to the measurement of impact concentrates attention upon 'important' decisions (the Committee's own term) and evaluates the role of political bodies or actors purely in relation to the relative part they play in causing specific changes to policies. It is not concerned with the long-term influences that a body of individuals may wield. Many Committee members, as we showed earlier in this chapter, feel that such indirect influences are all that they can realistically achieve. Now it must be clear from the examination of all the forces affecting the levels and patterns of public spending that were considered in Chapter One that no Government has an unfettered ability to make 'important' decisions about public spending being hemmed in by all manner of constraints. Its decisions are, moreover, largely incremental, forming part of clusters of decisions or of the development of policies. The Expenditure Committee, too, is rarely concerned with single 'important' decisions but mostly with investigating areas of policy. Even in cases where it has examined the anatomy of an individual decision—such as Trade and Industry's enquiry into financial support for British Leyland—the decision must be seen in relation to the general Governmental attitude towards support for failing industries. The work of other sub-committees such as Education and Arts, General, and Defence and External Affairs, have followed a sequential pattern, in which enquiries bear some relationship one to another. The Expenditure Committee's efforts should therefore not merely be measured in terms of immediate Governmental response, or lack of it. Its process of gathering evidence and making recommendations means that it is continually exposing the assumptions of decision makers, the limitations of their information, and the weaknesses of their judgement. Continual contact between the Committee and decision makers may eventually have some effect upon the latter. Indeed, examination of the relationship between the ideas presented to the Committee by its witnesses from outside Government, its recommendations and the Government's responses, yields a

[23] *First Special Report from the Expenditure Committee*, H.C. 68, 1975–76, p. 5.

general model of attitude transference that deserves closer examination. Witnesses from outside Government present novel and sometimes radical ideas to the sub-committee; it considers each in relation to all other evidence and produces an amalgam acceptable to its own members for its report. This amalgam will generally be too innovatory or radical for instant acceptance by Government but passes into the general stream of thought on the subject and may find later acceptance.

Measuring the alteration of attitudes of Government and Government officials is, however, even more difficult than trying to trace the effect of the Committee on individual decisions. It can only be done indirectly owing to the nature of the British civil service which does not expose itself to independent surveys of its attitudes and opinions. But some people do believe that the Select Committees of the House of Commons, through their very existence, affect the attitudes of the civil servants appearing before them. Robert Sheldon, then Financial Secretary to the Treasury, stated with respect to the Public Accounts Committee:

> The success of the Committee's work cannot and should not be measured by the attendance of Hon. Members in this House when the Reports are debated, but by the way in which it changes the future of those who appear before it, and changes the way Government operations are conducted.[24]

It is not easy for the Expenditure Committee of non-expert M.P.s to change the well entrenched attitudes of the 'top brass' of the civil service, and indeed few of the Permanent Secretaries are called before it to give evidence. Only when an enquiry is of a highly political nature, like those into *The Motor Vehicle Industry* and *Public Expenditure on Chrysler*, or related to judgements about policy such as the Expenditure White Papers or elements of Defence Policy, will Permanent Secretaries appear before sub-committees. Incidentally the 'Crossman' specialist Select Committees of 1966 did frequently call Ministers and Permanent Secretaries to give evidence and the Government of the day became concerned at the disruption this practice caused. Most of the civil servants appearing before the Expenditure Committee are Under-Secretaries and Assistants, and the burden of work on them can be absorbed without too much trouble. These men are those who will later move on to higher posts. Already some regular early witnesses to the Expenditure Committee have

[24] H.C. Debates, 22 January 1976, col. 1623.

reached the level of Permanent Secretary—Leo Pliatzky, for example. At the very least such men carry into their higher responsibilities an awareness that Parliament cannot be totally ignored.

An indirect measure of the effect of the Expenditure Committee on the attitudes of the civil service can be made by calculation of the work load that its existence creates in the Departments. Departments are asked to provide witnesses to give oral evidence, to prepare memoranda, and to reply to reports. It is not possible to be precise about how many men or how many man hours are involved in work for the Expenditure Committee. The Ministry of Defence has noted that with respect to the procedure of preparing observations on Committee recommendations it is not a practicable proposition to attempt an estimate of the numbers of civil servants engaged in such work.[25] This is probably another way of saying that the Department is not prepared to work out the estimate; the United States Government has calculated and published the number of man hours spent by its Department of Defense on legislative activities.[26]

Prior to the establishment of the Expenditure Committee in 1970

Table Ten   Number of Witnesses from Central Government Departments Giving Oral Evidence Before the Expenditure Committee, 1971–74 (February)

Department	*Number of civil servants giving evidence*						*Total number of appearances*
	Once	*Twice*	*Three times*	*Four times*	*Five times*	*Six+ times*	
Defence	69	15	4	4	1	1	94 (138)
Employment	24	10	1		2		37 (57)
Environment	23	3	5	1		1 (7 times)	33 (55)
Trade and Industry	13	5					18 (23)
Education	6	5	4		1	1 (9 times)	17 (41)
Treasury	10	2	2		1	1 (10 times)	16 (35)
Foreign Office	25		1				31 (38)
Health and Social Security	8	2	1				11 (16)
Home Office	5		4				9 (17)
Scottish and Welsh Office	5						5 (5)

[25] *Sixth Report from the Expenditure Committee*, H.C. 167 of 1973–74, p. 13.

[26] *Department of Defense Appropriation Bill 1976*, November 6 1975, *Report of the Committee on Appropriations*, Senate Calendar No. 432, 94th Congress, 1st Session, Report no. 94–446.

few Departments had close and frequent connections with Select Committees, though they sent witnesses from time to time to appear before the PAC, the Estimates Committee, and the 'Crossman' committees. The Expenditure Committee has greatly increased the two-way traffic between the civil service and the House of Commons. Only since 1971, when the Expenditure Committee began its work, have a number of Departments had to take regular note of the Committees of the House. Regular contacts, however, still do not extend to all Departments, as Tables Ten and Eleven show.

Table Eleven   Number of Witnesses from Central Government Departments Giving Oral Evidence Before the Expenditure Committee, 1974–76 (April)

Department	Number of civil servants giving evidence						Total number of appearances
	Once	Twice	Three times	Four times	Five times	Six+ times	
Defence	39	8	4	1			52 (71)
Employment	7		1				8 (10)
Environment	14	6	1	1	2	{ (1-6 times) (1-7 times)	24 (46)
Trade and Industry	13	2	2	2	2		21 (41)
Education	7		1	2	1		11 (23)
Treasury	24	5	4			4 { (2-6 times) (2-7 times) (1-9 times)	37 (68)
Foreign and Commonwealth Office	7	7	1			5	20 (49)
Health and Social Security	23	3	2	1		2 (2-7 times)	31 (46)
Home Office	14						14 (14)
Scottish and Welsh Offices	17						17 (17)
Inland Revenue, Customs and Excise	6						6 (6)
Agriculture and Fisheries	5						5 (5)
Prices and Consumer Protection	2						2 (2)

Note: The periods covered by Tables Ten and Eleven are almost identical in length. The Expenditure Committee began work at the start of 1971 and carried on in the same Parliament until February 1974 (a period of three years). The second period starts after the February 1974 election and continues till the end of the 1976 session (a period of two and a half years).

The burden of work imposed upon the Departments by the necessity of providing oral evidence to the Expenditure Committee varies from year to year and is in some cases dependent upon the calls of particular enquiries. Thus the figures for the Department of Employment in the period 1970–74 were swollen by the three enquiries of the Employment and Social Services sub-committee into aspects of the employment services; the Trade and Industry figures were increased in the period from 1974 by the two enquiries into aspects of the Government's subsidies to the motor industry; and in the same period the call made upon the Department of Health and Social Security was increased by the large enquiry by the Employment and Social Services sub-committee into *Preventive Medicine*. Once these particular causes for large demands are taken into account, it is clear that only a few Departments have a continuing (though relatively small) burden of evidence provision. They are the Departments that have sub-committees directly interested in their work—Defence, Treasury, Education, Trade and Industry and Environment. The amount of interaction between individual civil servants and the Expenditure Committee can be judged from the number of times any one person is called to give evidence. The vast majority only have to appear once before the Committee in any one Parliament. Only about one-third of those called have appeared more than once, and only between 5–10 per cent more than four times. The fact that a few have been called four, five or six times is related more to the relevance of their own work for a particular enquiry in hand than to their over-all close relationship with the Committee. Once that particular enquiry is over, these men may have no further contact with it. Thus the number of civil servants who can be said to have a regular and continuing contact through the provision of evidence is small. Only in the Treasury and in the Department of the Environment have there been in both periods a handful of men who have appeared frequently as witnesses. Civil servants called upon to give oral evidence do so as part of their general duties and are not especially assigned to Expenditure Committee work. In the Treasury, however, almost all of those providing oral evidence come from one group—the Public Expenditure Group—whose awareness of the Expenditure Committee is probably by this time more acute than that of any other group of civil servants either in that Department or in others.

The burden of work created through the need to provide written evidence involves a further number of civil servants. Most civil service memoranda produced for the Committee are, however, short, partly because British civil servants are by tradition accustomed to write short memoranda and partly because they, like most other witnesses, think that the Committee will not read anything long. The memoranda represented by the figures in Table Twelve vary in size from one or two hundred words to several thousand words. The great bulk of them however consist of one or two pages.

Table Twelve Memoranda Presented to the Expenditure Committee by Central Government Departments

Department		*Session*						
	1970–71	1971–72	1972–73	1973–73	1974	1974–75	1975–76	Totals
Defence		15	6	15	14	15	65	130
Employment	5		16	1	2	3	1	28
Environment		3	46*	2	3	39	7	100
Trade and Industry		8	11	4		10	11	44
Education	5		6	5	16	3	9	44
Treasury	14	8	9	2	3	23	5	64
Foreign Office		2	1		12	14		29
Health and Social Security		14	6	9	2	11	6	48
Home Office		7			5	5		17
Scottish and Welsh Offices	2	5	7	2		1	3	20
Housing							1	1
Inland Revenue, Customs and Excise							3	3
Agriculture and Fisheries					10			10
Energy					1			1
Totals	21	67	108	40	58	134	110	529

* Of this total 32 memoranda were to the enquiry on *Urban Transport Planning* and 13 on *Home Improvement Grants*.

Although the number of civil servants who have been engaged at one time or another in work caused by the Expenditure Committee runs into hundreds and represents a substantial increase in the two-way traffic between Parliament and Whitehall, the figures need to be looked at in perspective if we are to use them to evaluate the degree of influence over the minds of civil servants that this increased contact can create. An average of twenty Ministry of Defence staff (some being servicemen working in the Ministry) appear before the Expenditure Committee in any one year. Compare this with the United States Defense Department which in 1974 alone sent 870 witnesses (plus many others as observers) to testimony sessions before Congressional Committees concerned with the budgetary process.

One result of the intermittent nature of the burden of evidence provision falling upon the Departments is that few have seen the need to make concerted efforts to set up special organisations to cope with calls made upon them by the Committee. Each Department has an official designated as liaison officer, and he is the one who normally calls upon civil servants working in areas relevant to an enquiry to act as witnesses. In a few cases a sub-committee asks for individual civil servants by name—as for example when it wishes to question a Permanent Secretary. In the Foreign Office the liaison officer has the additional task of making arrangements whenever any of the sub-committees decide to travel abroad. Only in the Ministry of Defence does this official have a small staff, some of whom spend a considerable amount of their time on Expenditure Committee work. In all other Departments, including the Foreign Office, the official has to combine his liaison work with other duties. A few sub-committees admittedly have informal links with other, higher ranks, as the Expenditure Committee chairman, James Boyden, has indicated:

> It is rather unusual to mention civil servants by name in the House, but I should like to refer to the contribution made by the late Sir Michael Cary, whose death was a great blow to the country and to the Ministry of Defence, and not least to the Expenditure Committee. He established the most excellent personal relations with the Defence sub-committee of the Expenditure Committee. He convened conferences between the Committee and his leading officials to iron out difficulties.[27]

The infrequency and irregularity of contacts between high-level civil servants and most sub-committees, however, is responsible for many of the complaints made about the lack of impact that the Committee has. It is just one of many reasons leading to the conclusion that the Committee has had but marginal influence upon the attitudes and biases of the civil service.

There is the possibility that new ideas will percolate from the Expenditure Committee to the Government in an indirect way through

[27] H.C. Debates, 13 April 1976, col. 1230.

the medium of debate on the floor of the House. One of the original expectations of the Expenditure Committee, indeed, was that it would influence Government through this route. Examination of the contents of the special debates held on the reports of the Committee, and of the use made of information from Committee reports in other debates, reveals how little this expectation of its impact has been fulfilled. As Table Thirteen shows, there were nine debates on Committee reports between the time of its establishment in 1970 and the end of the 1975–76 session.

Table Thirteen   Debates on Expenditure Committee Reports

Title of report	Date of public-action	Date of debate	Delay in months between publication and debate	Total time
Probation and After Care	16.12.71	9.2.71	3	2hr 10m
Defence and External Affairs	2.2.72	7.8.72	6	4hr 45m
Urban Transport Planning	18.1.73	9.7.73	6	2hr 31m
Further and Higher Education	20.12.72	9.7.73	8	2hr 7m
Employment (3 reports)	8.4.73	15.1.74	9	2hr 28m
	12.4.73		9	
	10.6.73		7	
Public Expenditure on Transport	17.7.74	1.6.75	11	2hr 6m
Police Recruitment and Wastage	24.7.74	1.6.75	11	2hr 26m
Postgraduate Education	20.12.73	10.7.75	(19)	3hr 6m
Education Maintenance Allowances	24.7.74		(12)	
Children and Young Persons Act	7.7.75	13.4.76	9	5hr 22m

A total of 27 hours of debating time were thus devoted to the output of the Committee, an average of 4 hours to discuss the ten or so reports published each year. Most of the reports, of course, were never discussed at all. Of the nine debates all but two (in the session 1971–72) took place on Supply Days, because Governments were unwilling to grant any of their own time for this purpose. The debates attracted sparse attendance—there were complaints about the emptiness of the House during the Employment debate on 15 January 1974. A disproportionate number of speakers were themselves Committee members. The other speakers were for the most part attracted to the debates more for the opportunities they gave them to press constituency matters than for the chance to analyse the contents of the Committee's reports. Thus in the debate on *Urban Transport Planning* in July 1973 Arthur Palmer spoke of Bristols traffic problems and of the planning blight accompanying the city's as yet unrealised plans for an inner ring urban motorway. Sydney Chapman said Birmingham proved the theory that more roads meant more cars. Peter Doig (a Member for Dundee) praised motorways because they made Scotland more accessible.

The debates that have taken place have occurred months, in some cases even a year or more, after the publication of a report—indeed the time lapses between the publication of a report and debate in the House seem in recent years to have increased rather than decreased. The delay in debating reports is clearly linked to the Government's unwillingness to produce observations within a reasonable timespan, and Committee members have made many complaints about this both in debates and in special reports, notably the one published on 11 December 1975. On two occasions[28] a debate has taken place without the benefit of any Government observations. The irritation felt because of Government delay was most clearly expressed by James Boyden during the 1976 debate on *The Children and Young Persons' Act 1969*. Earlier that day, he said, it has been necessary for Mr William Whitelaw to question the Prime Minister about the 'overlong delay in making a reply to the Committee'. He continued:

> It should not be necessary to bother the Prime Minister or for the right Hon. Member for Penrith and the Border to have to raise the matter in the House, when it should be standard drill for the Departments to react reasonably quickly and with reasonable competence on the recommendations that are made.

[28] Debates on *Probation and After Care* (9 February 1972) and on *The Children and Young Persons' Act 1969* (13 April 1976).

Two Departments which are not generally considered absolutely outrageously speedy, the Ministry of Defence, and the Treasury, find these days that they are well able to deal with Reports of the Expenditure Committee most expeditiously.... Therefore, in two of the Major Departments of State there are good relations, especially in relation to the speed of answering the Committee's reports, and excellent relations have been established.

On the other hand there are Departments that are very unsatisfactory in this respect. The Department of Education and Science has two reports that are two years outstanding for Departmental Observations.... There need not be delays at all, because Departments appoint liaison officers to these Committees. In this case there was an officer from the Home Office and one from the Department of Education and Science.[29]

And Mark Carlisle noted that other bodies apart from the Expenditure Committee had their own difficulties in obtaining reactions from the Government about the issue of juvenile offenders:

I was horrified to learn today that since January of this year the chairmen of the inner London juvenile courts have been attempting without success to obtain a meeting with the Minister in the Department of Health and Social Security to discuss the Children and Young Persons Act.[30]

This particular debate was better attended than most, was longer and attracted better speeches (even though, as Members noted, there was no Government representative in the House for most of the time to listen to them). The reason for the interest aroused by the debate was that it was on a subject only marginally connected with public spending—being about the keeping of children in prison for want of more suitable correction centres—which had, owing to one or two notable cases of young girls placed in Holloway Gaol, caused public concern. Debates that attract attention do so not for the public spending matters that they raise but for the opportunity to debate a policy area of special interest to a small group of Members. It is notable that the two sub-committees which are said to enjoy 'good relations' with their Departments and which tend to examine matters of technical and financial rather than of political interest, have not, with the exception of one debate on Defence in 1972, had their reports debated. Neither has the Trade and Industry sub-committee had a report debated—indeed, its first chairman indicated that he was aiming for other channels of influence than the Chamber of the

[29] H.C. Debates, 13 April 1976, cols. 1229–1231.
[30] *Ibid*, col. 1263.

House of Commons. Of the nine debates between 1972 and 1976 four were on reports from the Environment sub-committee, two were from Education and Arts, and two from Employment and Social Services.

Even when they have finally wrung observations from a reluctant Department, Members sometimes express dissatisfaction with the lack of positive action promised. In the debate on *Urban Transport Planning* John Horam complained that it was not clear from the observations what action the Government intended to take, even though it had expressed general agreement with the sentiments of the report.

> The section (of the Government Observations) dealing with the role of the Central Government ... is a bundle of platitudes. It says, for example, that we should not be concerned with details.... We want to know what the Government are doing about this and what broad policy they have.... Only at the end of this section is there a limp statement that the Secretary of State hoped that in future local authorities would pay greater attention to helping public transport and restraining the car.... It is no good having Select Committees as industrious as this Select Committee, White Papers which are welcoming and helpful, and encouraging Ministerial speeches if in the end there is very little change.[31]

A similar complaint was made in a Defence debate (note, not on an Expenditure Committee report) when James Boyden charged the Ministry with inaction over married service quarters in Gibraltar. This was said of a Department that does at least produce its observations: 'The Committee visited Gibraltar eighteen months ago and drew attention to the extremely unsatisfactory state of the building of married quarters. Despite the 360 (sic) papers and the many witnesses from the Ministry of Defence nothing very much happened.' The sub-committee therefore tried the direct approach so often used by M.P.s who wish to influence Ministers: 'However, the Defence Committee was in Gibraltar last week, and yesterday the Hon. and Gallant Member for Eye and myself saw the Minister of State, and it is to be hoped that some action will now result.[32]

Only rarely do Members, as in the debate on Defence quoted from above, refer to the work of the Expenditure Committee on any but the special occasions for considering its reports. It rarely gets a mention in Defence debates, for example, perhaps for the reason that these are on extremely broad subjects such as 'The Army' or 'The Navy', and are occasion for broad policy clashes rather than for detailed

---

[31] H.C. Debates, 9 July 1971, col. 1102.
[32] H.C. Debates, 2 July 1974, col. 265.

consideration of financial provision. There is no evidence that committee members have contributed more than proportionately to debates on expenditure topics which are related in a general way to their sub-committee terms of reference and in which they might be expected to have gained some expertise.[33] The one significant occasion when material from an Expenditure Committee report was used was the debate on 16 December 1975 on the motor industry (on a motion to reduce the salary of the Secretary of State for Industry). As usual the Minister of State had to apologise for not having produced a Government reply to the Trade and Industry sub-committee's report on *The Motor Vehicle Industry*. The report itself proved a useful source of information for those M.P.s wishing to criticise the Government. Some quoted from the report directly—an unusual event in references to the Expenditure Committee's work. There were two other main sources of information available to M.P.s (the Central Policy Review Staff's report on the motor industry, and the Ryder Report on British Leyland). But the Committee's report was the document singled out for special praise: 'However, even the CPRS report fails to put the matter into anything like the full context provided by the report of the Select Committee'.[34] With the exception of this report there is no evidence that any work produced by the Expenditure Committee in six years has contributed significantly to any single House of Commons debate (other than the nine quoted in Table Thirteen above, which are a special category). A more indirect contribution—through Members reading the reports or press coverage of the reports—cannot, however, be ruled out.

One last expectation of the Expenditure Committee was that it would provide a two-way information link between Government and people. To estimate the degree of influence it wields through the publicity it attracts is exceptionally difficult for the reason that it is really six separate Committees each with its own public. Something can at least be said about public awareness of the Committee's work. Measured by the number of the general public attending evidence sessions, or coming forward as individuals to give evidence, this awareness is very limited. The individuals most aware of the Committee are usually in pressure groups. The Committee for its part has made some effort to publicise its activities. Notices of forthcoming evidence

---

[33] An analysis has been made of the speakers in debates on expenditure subjects from 1970 to 1974 which reveals no clear correlation between participation in expenditure-related debates and membership of the Expenditure Committee.

[34] Richard Wainwright, H.C. Debates, 16 December 1975, col. 1235.

sessions and names of witnesses scheduled to appear are published each week in *The Times* and *The Daily Telegraph* together with other Parliamentary notices. From 1975 notices of Select Committee meetings have also appeared on the daily House of Commons Order Paper (which shows the order of Parliamentary business). Order Papers are circulated to all M.P.s and are also available to the Press. It is a pity that Select Committee meetings are not also advertised in newspapers each morning together with information of the room location. And a more convenient meeting place than the Committee Corridor might encourage better attendance—gaining access to the meetings of the Expenditure Committee is like tackling an obstacle course.

The Committee's evidence sessions are open to the press (with the exception of those heard in private which include almost all of the Defence sub-committee's sessions). However the general lobby correspondents assigned to Westminster rarely pay much interest, save when an enquiry is on a really 'political' subject. They prefer the more dramatic scenes on the floor of the House and the intrigues of the corridors. Most of the journalists present at evidence sessions come from the specialist press: financial journalists from the City and the business pages of *The Times*, *The Daily Telegraph*, and *The Financial Times*, cover the work of the General sub-committee; Education correspondents from both the daily press and the educational weeklies attend Education and Arts; and so on. Defence is the only sub-committee which, because of the privacy of its hearings, cannot have a regular press following, although its reports are covered in specialist magazines like *Brasseys*. The result of this press coverage is a trickle of news about the witnesses and the evidence they supply to the Committee in the more serious dailies and periodicals. Whether broadcasting of the proceedings will, when it is introduced on a regular basis, increase public awareness of the work of Select Committees remains uncertain. The specialist nature of the Committee's activities is not likely to appeal to other than specialist audiences. However the Expenditure Committee, early in its life, thought that broadcasting would increase public awareness. In its *Second Special Report* of 1972–73 it asked the House to authorise broadcasting of its public proceedings.

More obvious publicity may be achieved when the Committee issues a report. If it is of sufficient importance, a press conference is held. This may result in wide coverage, especially if the report has more than a little political content. Reports that have received this treatment include: *Wages and Conditions of African Workers; National*

Health Facilities for Private Patients; Public Expenditure, Inflation and the Balance of Payments; and *The Civil Service.* This last, skilfully issued during the Parliamentary recess when there was little other Parliamentary news of interest, was the front page lead story in *The Times.* Following the successful launching of a report, a sub-committee chairman may find himself being interviewed for radio and television news programmes. Such publicity reveals, although in an ephemeral manner, the general thrust of a committee's recommendations. It cannot display though the full argument of the report or the evidence on which the recommendations were based. In a few cases the more serious newspapers publish a section of a report, as *The Times* did on 16 September 1977 with the report on *The Civil Service.* This is the nearest that most of the public, and most M.P.s, get to reading through a report of the Expenditure Committee. Most of the copies printed, of which about one to two thousand are sold, are purchased by libraries from whence they rarely issue.

As one Committee member has commented, 'Good administration is not newsworthy'.[35] This is precisely the Expenditure Committee's dilemma with respect to publicity. If it opts for 'political' subjects or allows party differences to intrude, it will achieve, perhaps only short-lived, public impact. If it devotes its efforts to analysis of Government spending plans in detail and to the development of policy options and alternatives for more efficient and effective use of public money, it is unlikely to have a wide appeal. When the Committee has examined priorities in public spending, it gets little notice. Its report of the 1976–77 session on *Select Public Expenditure Programmes* in which each sub-committee examined a section of the Public Expenditure White Paper appeared on 30 June 1977 without a major stir. The basic problem with the Expenditure Committee is that it has simply to rely upon influence; it has no powers over expenditure. If however it were given some actual powers of decision making over public spending, as are the Budget Committees of the US Congress, such analytical and financial material would immediately become a much greater object of public attention.

---

[35] James Boyden, H.C. Debates, 13 April 1976, col. 1234.

8 A New View of Parliament's Power of the Purse

It does not seem, on balance of the evidence presented in the foregoing chapters, that the Expenditure Committee has fulfilled many of the expectations held out for it. It has done a great deal of work. Its sub-committees together have interviewed over 2000 witnesses and produced hundreds of pages of recommendations. But for all this it cannot claim to have had either much concrete impact upon Government decisions about public spending or more than a limited amount of influence on the policy making process. It has not fulfilled Mr Peart's fears that it would be a 'radical and coherent approach to the balance of power between the House and the Executive' and tip that balance in favour of the House. It has certainly not revived Parliament's traditional power of the purse. One reason for this is that it has operated too much like the Estimates Committee that it replaced to provide a 'radical and coherent' change. The power relationships between Parliament and the Executive remain essentially what they were before the establishment of the Committee, although tempered somewhat in the period from February 1974 by the circumstances of minority Government. As for its influence, that too must be regarded as limited in the absence of evidence to the contrary. Certainly the Committee has increased the flow of information from the civil service to Parliament and between pressure groups and Parliament to some extent. Its enquiries have also revealed something of the processes by which the Government makes decisions about public spending. But its influence on Members of Parliament other than its own membership is slight. David Howell's and others' hopes that the Expenditure Committee would lead to more lively and informed debates on the floor of the House of Commons have scarcely been fulfilled; there are few occasions when its work is even mentioned on the floor of the House.

The experience of the first six years of the Expenditure Committee gives the impression that if it wanted to become a more influential instrument in the process of determining public spending, then its members would have to work even harder than they do at present on its sub-committees. They would have to prepare themselves to become more efficient questioners of the witnesses and more effective probers of the assumptions and figures behind the Government's expenditure plans. Secondly, the Committee would need to change its style of working, moving away from the studies of particular items and policies which it has been so fond of, and instead concentrating on critical examination in depth of the actual spending plans laid before Parliament by the Government in its White Papers. It would need to consider those plans in the light of possible alternatives and options. In order to do this, it would need to ensure some degree of integration between the work of the sub-committees so that expenditure on one function of Government could be examined in relation to expenditure on others. There is no way at present for the Committee to produce a reasoned argument that, for example, more money spent on Defence means less spent on Health or on Education. Finally, the Committee would have to learn how to collect information in a more systematic fashion, to relate that information more closely to expenditure and the effects of expenditure, and to approach its material in a more analytical fashion. For this task it would need a staff equipped to analyse the Government's proposals and to evaluate alternatives. It is significant that some, at least, of the Expenditure Committee's membership have always been aware of these needs. In its *Second Special Report* of 1970–1971 the Committee asked that it be given a secretariat to help it with analysis, and six years later it made the same point in its report on *The Civil Service* (issued in August 1977). There is, however, no clear perception of these conditions for successful influence among all Expenditure Committee members, and as a result there has been no impetus for it to follow them.

Even if all the conditions for success were to be fulfilled, if the Committee were to become more active and co-ordinated with a staff of its own, how much greater would its influence on Government really be? Could it ever become more than a minor irritant on the Government's skin? The major impediments that prevent the Expenditure Committee from becoming more influential stem not only from the inclinations and behaviour of its own membership, although these are significant, but also from the underlying forces that structure the general patterns of attitudes and behaviour among British Members of Parliament. These forces, which are interrelated, are the fusion of powers in the constitution between the Legislature and the Executive, and the strong disciplined party system. The constitutional and political settings in which the Expenditure Committee operates provide the main stumbling blocks to its greater effectiveness.

The constitutional fusion of powers in the United Kingdom between the Legislature and the Executive conditions everything that Members of Parliament do. They cannot escape from the fact that the British House of Commons is more than a representative assembly—it is also a recruiting ground for Government ministers. Members of Parliament are representatives of their constituents, certainly, and much of their behaviour is directed towards fulfilling their representative role. But they are also apprentices in the workshop of master administrators and their attitude towards Government and party leadership, and their subsequent behaviour, is coloured and shaped by the need to promote their own political careers. Only very rarely does anyone become a Minister without serving a pretty lengthy apprenticeship in the House of Commons. M.P.s are thus locked into a career structure within the assembly. Moreover, the front benchers who are instrumental in the promotion of junior Members of their parties do not attend Select Committees and so these arenas have little significance in terms of members' career ambitions.

The Government's view of the constitution has also affected Members' behaviour. Governments have come to interpret the fusion of powers as meaning that any deviation from the proposals that they lay before Parliament puts their tenure in office at risk. They believe that rejection of their Bills means rejection of the Government. They therefore expect that the Bills they introduce will pass through the House of Commons virtually unchanged except in insignificant details. They cannot accept that some, non-Government Members of Parliament, might know better than the Government what policies should be adopted in particular circumstances. In the case of Appropriations Bills (granting Supply) no changes are permitted at all. This attitude on behalf of Government with respect to public spending proposals has been accepted by the House of Commons for many years, so that the fiction of Parliament's power of the purse has come to be known for what it is. Unless Governments are able to interpret the British Constitution in a different way so as to allow the Expenditure Committee (or any other designated Committee of the House of Commons) to vote upon and alter details of the Estimates and of the Public Expenditure White Papers, or unless some more dramatic change in the constitution providing a separation of Executive and Legislative powers occurs, Parliament's power or influence over public spending can not be increased by anything more than the most minute degree. The Expenditure Committee can work as hard as it likes, but it can achieve no greater impact under the present distribution of powers in the constitution.

Connected with, and flowing from, the constitutional provision of fusion of powers, is the strong party system that has developed in the British Parliament. The strong party system is supposed by some to have its roots in the divided class system of British society, and by others to be caused by the British electoral system. Whatever the causes of the two party system outside Parliament might be, it must be recognised that the fusion of powers in the constitution is an underlying bulwark of that strong party system and helps to maintain it. Every tactic and rule of the Parliamentary parties is drawn up with the need to support the Government (and the Opposition) in mind. The whole structure of party organisation and the system of whipping, together with changes in procedure during the past 100 years, have been developed to ensure that a Government once elected remains in office and achieves its legislative programme. The tight party system ensures that M.P.s vote as they are told, rather than as a rational consideration of facts might dictate. This party system is at odds, therefore, with any system of Parliamentary scrutiny of public spending which allows small committees of men working together on evaluation of public spending proposals to consider alternatives to the Government's plans. So long as the strong party system has such a hold over the minds of British politicians, it is unlikely that they will allow the Expenditure Committee the power to vote upon and to make decisions about public spending. And yet, without that power, it cannot advance. Only if the party system were to loosen its grip upon the minds of Members could they assert their individual opinions on matters of public spending in a rational manner and without fear that loss of a vote in the House would lead to the downfall of their Government. As it is, the present system of fusion of powers linked with strong disciplined parties is perfectly tuned to support a reforming Government that wants to pass radical and novel legislation and to play out what has been called 'adversary politics'. It is not adapted to cool and rational appraisal of alternatives and options in a situation where public spending is already so great that not new programmes but more effective ones are required. Now that the Government spends more than half of the national output each year, there is an urgent need for Parliament to concern itself with 'value for money'. But so long as no committee or any other Parliamentary body is to be allowed to alter a single penny of the Government's expenditure plans, Parliament must remain essentially impotent in respect to the control of public spending.

But even if the House of Commons were to be given the power to alter Governments' spending proposals, how far would this enhance its role in the determination of public spending in Britain? As we showed in Chapter One, there are many forces at work in the determination of public spending patterns. Economic pressures, social forces, historical experience and political power all play their part in shaping the final pattern of public spending. It is not only unrealistic to think of Parliament as having ultimate power over public spending; it is also unrealistic to think of the Central Government as the final determinator of spending, for, when making its decisions, Central Government responds to the demands of many bodies including local authorities, hospital boards, universities, and trades unions. Some of these bodies have a direct line of access to Downing Street and Whitehall. Even international forces are significant influences on Expenditure decisions. In 1976 and 1977 one major constraint on the Government's spending and budgetary decisions was the International Monetary Fund. In return for a loan, which was essential at the time, the Fund imposed certain conditions about the growth of public spending and the expansion of the public sector borrowing requirement. In the years from 1974 the TUC has been another important influence upon the Government— demanding, for example, the maintenance of what it has called 'the social wage' (i.e. public spending) in return for a commitment on its part to restrain wage demands. These two forces together have meant that the Government has been torn between the need to cut the expansion in public spending to meet the conditions of the IMF and the need to maintain high levels of spending as demanded by the TUC. This example helps to demonstrate how the Government is not a free agent in determining the total levels of public spending.

Not only does the Government find itself constrained by external forces when making its decisions about spending; it also finds it has only limited control over the actual amounts of money spent. Experience has shown that the actual amounts spent rarely correspond to the amounts that the Government wished to spend. One reason for this is that the Central Government is not the sole spender of public money in Britain. About one-third of all public spending is directly controlled by the local authorities. Part of this money (two-thirds) does come from the Central Government in the form of the Rate Support Grant. Once this is given over to the local authorities, however, they, not the Central Government, determine the detailed distribution of the money. Central Government has only limited means of determining precisely on what and how these bodies spend their funds. The grasp that it has over the disbursement of public funds is often extremely weak, and sometimes virtually non-existent. In other words it can be no more than a general pattern setter and a general overseer and broker. It can set certain targets and can pull and push economic levers to induce the economy to move in particular directions, although it is by no means certain that the movement of these levers will have the effects intended. Attempts to control spending more effectively through the Public Expenditure Survey Committee (PESC) from 1961 are now generally regarded as a failure, and the experience of 'cash limits' from 1976 which have created a new problem of 'shortfall' (underspending), demonstrates the limitations of the Central Government's power.[1]

It is therefore quite unrealistic to think of the Government as the sole determinant of public spending and of Parliament as the ultimate democratic check and control over that Central Government. Parliament must be seen in a more realistic light as one of a number of bodies with more or less influence in a complex process. Perhaps the economists are right after all; public spending levels are determined by economic forces. Or perhaps the social thinkers are right; society as a whole determines public spending. Perhaps the historians are right to point out the importance of historical precedents in determining spending patterns. Certainly there is no one answer to the question of how public spending is determined. What is clear is that Governments do not make these decisions alone, and Parliament does not hold the purse strings alone. Any procedural and constitutional changes that Parliament might achieve in future to enhance its relative position in the political system will not raise it up to a pre-eminent position above all other considerations. When, a century ago, Governments spent little on few objects, then it was reasonable to expect that an elected assembly could exercise some oversight and control over what was spent. When a Government spends, as it now does, as much as 50 per cent of the national income on a wide variety of functions provided by a loosely structured delivery system, then no one can realistically expect that even the best organised and best serviced legislature could exert much detailed control. All that the House of Commons can hope

---

[1] For the problems of the PESC system, see M. Wright, 'Public Expenditure in Britain: The Crisis of Control', *Public Administration*, 55 (1977), 143–70. On shortfall, see Terry Ward, 'Cash Limits and the Shortfall in Public Spending', *The Times*, 3 October 1977.

for is to be one influence among the many impinging on the process of determining public spending.

The trouble with the House of Commons, as we have tried to demonstrate, is that it does not even do its limited job of influencing the Government very well. It has abandoned the use of practices and procedures that might assist it, and has made only limited use of the new procedures introduced in the expectation that they would in some way enhance the role of Parliament. To say that it does not do even its limited job very well is not necessarily to criticise those individual M.P.s who have tried hard since 1970 to play a full role in the work of the Expenditure Committee (although they do not seem to have moved in the right directions) or to accuse other Members of slackness or incompetence. There are just too many institutional and attitudinal barriers to an extension of Parliamentary influence. Before we bear down too critically on the weaknesses and failures of the Expenditure Committee as a procedural innovation, we must recognise that the constitutional and political constraints under which it operates ensured from the start that it would never fulfil the greatest expectations of it—that it could redress the balance of power between Executive and Legislature. It is perhaps remarkable that the Committee has done as well as it has, for it faces Government Ministers whose attitude to Parliament's power over spending is not far from the attitude expressed by Bolingbroke in the quotation at the start of Chapter One. Denzil Davies, Minister of State at the Treasury, stated in a debate on 15 July 1977:

> I am sure that the Hon. Gentleman will agree that the House cannot determine expenditure of £16,000 on the purchase of typewriters.... The Hon. Gentleman has raised a case that illustrates the difficulty in any modern complex society of exercising detailed control over a bureaucracy. Bureaucracy is not necessarily a bad thing, but there is difficulty in controlling detailed Government expenditure. However, I must repeat that at the end of the day Parliament has the authority and the power to control Government Expenditure. It can deny that Government money, and if that happens to any Government they must hand over to somebody else.[2]

Ministers can make such pronouncements while Governments rest assured that these powers will never be used. The power that Davies speaks of is as meaningless as the Queen's power to refuse Royal Assent to Bills, as the Canadian Governor General's power to disallow Provincial legislation, and as the European Parliament's power to

[2] H.C. Debates, 15 July 1977, col. 1116.

dismiss the Commission of the European Communities. Exercise of such powers would have such serious repercussions upon the person exercising them that it is in effect no power at all. Even the threat of exercising the power is hollow. What Parliament needs is not a hollow power of life or death, but a little larger share in the process of deciding who gets what of public spending in Britain. The House of Commons will only get a larger share of power and influence when political attitudes towards the respective roles of Executive and Legislature change.

Appendix A
A Note on the Research

In addition to the analysis of documentary material reported in the text a number of interviews with members and ex-members of the Expenditure Committee were held between the end of 1973 and the start of 1975. Altogether 37 M.P.s provided formal interviews, 2 who had lost their seats in the February 1974 election replied by post, and several others have informally provided information since 1975. The interviews were considerably disrupted by the two elections of 1974 which took place in the middle of the interview period covered by the Social Science Research Council grant supporting this study. Members who then retired, or lost their seats, or became Ministers were less readily available than they had been prior to February 1974. Nevertheless very few of those approached refused to give interviews, and those who did generally acted on the grounds that they had been on the Committee for such a short period of time that they knew very little about its operations.

As is common in studies of legislative committees in the United States, the interviews were semi-structured (see R. Fenno, *Congressmen in Committees*, Little Brown, Boston, 1973, Introduction, p. xvi). The questions were presented in as informal a manner as possible in order to obtain the maximum amount of comment from respondents. Interviews varied in time from 20 minutes to several hours. The average time to complete all the necessary questions was about one hour. A set of questions was prepared to which answers were sought at some time during the conversation. Members were asked how they had joined the Committee (whether they had requested membership or whether they were approached by the Whips or any other persons); what their previous interest in Expenditure had been; what their personal contribution was to the work of the Committee (specifically their individual contribution to the selection of the topics studied, the selection of information and witnesses, the writing of the report); what their impressions of and relationship to the specialist adviser were;

what they thought of the impact of the Committee on the Government, the House of Commons, the Press and the Public; and finally what their views were on the role of Select Committees in general and on the relationship of Parliament to the Executive. In later interviews, as a result of comments from those interviewed earlier, Members' ideas were also sought on the amount of help and research assistance they considered desirable for successful Select Committee work. They were also asked how much time they devoted to the Expenditure Committee and the relationship of this work to their other Parliamentary duties. All the interviews were conducted on the basis that respondents would not be identified by name in any resulting publication. Quotations in the text from interviews are generally identified only by reference to the sub-committee membership of the respondent, although occasionally the party affiliation is also indicated.

Interviews were also held with ten clerks of the House of Commons, ten civil servants, and five specialist advisers. The clerks and advisers have continued to provide information in the period from 1975. Discussions with the clerks were mainly concerned with discovering the mechanics of Select Committee work and those with the civil servants (mainly Departmental liaison officers) with discovering the amount and nature of the work created in the Departments by the existence of the Expenditure Committee.

One piece of empirical research was carried out in respect of the witnesses to the Expenditure Committee (see above, page 124 ff.). A copy of the questionnaire sent to the staff members of the University of Bath and to the non-medical staff of University College, Cardiff, is reproduced below (pages 164–5).

Please answer the questions below by ticking the appropriate box and writing in as necessary.

Q.1. The Education and Arts Sub-Committee of the House of Commons Expenditure Committee has been carrying out an enquiry during the last year. Have you heard of the topic of that enquiry?

If YES, would you write in below what you have heard that topic to be.

NO   1

YES   2   (Write in)

Q.2. Which of these teaching duties does your post involve you in?

Teaching undergraduates	1	
Teaching other non-degree courses	2	
Teaching post-graduate course work	3	
Supervising post-graduate research	4	
Other (please detail here)	5	

Q.3.   Which of these newspapers and magazines do you read or look
       at regularly (that is, for daily papers at least four out of every
       six copies, for weeklies at least two out of every four copies)?

   Daily

               The Times   1 ▢
               Guardian   2 ▢
               Telegraph   3 ▢

   Weekly

               Times Higher Education Supplement 1 ▢
               Times Education Supplement   2 ▢
               Spectator   3 ▢
               New Statesman   4 ▢
               New Scientist   5 ▢
               Sunday Times   6 ▢
               The Observer   7 ▢

Appendix B
List of Expenditure
Committee Reports

General Sub-Committee

Session 1970–71
    H.C. 549   *Command Papers on Public Expenditure*
Session 1971–72
    H.C. 62   *Changes in Public Expenditure*
    H.C. 450   *Public Expenditure and Economic Management*
    H.C. 515   *Relation of Expenditure to Needs*
Session 1972–73
    H.C. 209   *Revision of the Form of the Supply Estimates*
    H.C. 398   *The May 21st Expenditure Cuts*
    H.C. 149   *The White Paper 'Public Expenditure to 1976–77',*
                Cmnd 5158

    (H.C. 226–i ⎫
    (H.C. 467 ⎬ Minutes of Evidence only)

Session 1973–74
    (H.C. 143   Minutes of Evidence only: *Public Expenditure to*
                1977–78 Cmnd 5519, Public Expenditure and the
                Balance of Resources)

    (H.C. 53   Minutes of Evidence only)
Session 1974
    H.C. 328   *Public Expenditure, Inflation and the Balance of*
                Payments

    (H.C. 166   Minutes of Evidence only: *Contingencies Fund)*
Session 1974–75
    H.C. 278   *The White Paper 'Public Expenditure to 1978–79',*
                Cmnd 5879

    H.C. 106   *The Estimates of Public Expenditure for 1974–75*
    H.C. 474   *The Public Expenditure Implications of the April 1975*
                Budget
    H.C. 535   *Cash Limit Control of Public Expenditure*

Session 1975–76
H.C. 299   *The White Paper 'Public Expenditure to 1979–80', Cmnd 6393*
H.C. 69   *The Financing of Public Expenditure*
(H.C. 622   Evidence only: *The Chancellor's statement of 22 July 1976)*
H.C. 718   *Planning and Control of Public Expenditure*
Session 1976–77
H.C. 535–1   *The Civil Service*
H.C. 258   *White Paper on the Government Expenditure Plans, Cmnd 6721*

Defence and External Affairs Sub-Committee

Session 1971–72
H.C. 141   *2nd Report from the Expenditure Committee*
H.C. 344   *Diplomatic Staff and Overseas Accommodation*
H.C. 516   *9th Report from the Expenditure Committee*
Session 1972–73
H.C. 147   *Gibraltar*
H.C. 296   *Visit by the Defence and External Affairs Sub-Committee to Ottawa and Washington*
H.C. 399   *Nuclear Weapons Programme*
Session 1973–74
H.C. 29   *Accommodation and Staffing in Ottawa and Washington*
H.C. 167   *Review of Previous Defence Recommendations*
H.C. 168   *Defence Medical Services*
H.C. 99   *Multi Role Combat Aircraft*
H.C. 169   *Defence Expenditure*
Session 1974
H.C. 308   *Defence Cuts*
H.C. 309   *Service Married Quarters in Gibraltar*
H.C. 175   *The Cruiser Programme*
Session 1974–75
H.C. 259   *The Defence Review Proposals*
H.C. 220   *Central Management of the Services*
H.C. 472   *British Forces Germany*
H.C. 471   *Review of Previous Defence Recommendations*
H.C. 473   *Diplomatic Manpower and Property Overseas*

Session 1975–76
(H.C. 139	Evidence only: *H.M. Naval Base and H.M. Dock-yard Devonport*)
H.C. 431	*Defence Policy After the Review*
H.C. 155	*Defence*
H.C. 270	*Hong Kong and Cyprus*
H.C. 604	*Diplomatic Manpower and Property Overseas 1976 Review*
H.C. 696	*Visit to Canada and the United States*
H.C. 695	*Defence Medical Services*
H.C. 597	*Guided Weapons*

Session 1976–77
H.C. 392	*Progress towards Implementation of the Final Act of the Conference on Security in Co-operation in Europe*
H.C. 254	*Cumulative Effects of Cuts in Defence Expenditure*
H.C. 393	*Reserves and Reinforcements*

Trade and Industry Sub-Committee

Session 1971–72
H.C. 347	*Public Money in the Private Sector*

Session 1973–74
H.C. 85	*Regional Development Incentives*
H.C. 116	*Wages and Conditions of African Workers Employed by British Firms in South Africa*

Session 1974
H.C. 311	*Milk Production*

Session 1974–75
H.C. 617	*The Motor Vehicle Industry*

Session 1975–76
H.C. 596	*Public Expenditure on Chrysler U.K. Ltd*

Session 1976–77
H.C. 255	*Inquiry into the Fishing Industry—Progress Report*

Education and Arts Sub-Committee

Session 1970–71
H.C. 545	*Public Expenditure in Britain on Education Arts and Research Councils*

Session 1972–73
H.C. 48	*Further and Higher Education*

Session 1973–74
  H.C. 96   *Postgraduate Education*
Session 1974
  H.C. 306   *Education Maintenance Allowances in the 16–18 years*
                  Age Group
Session 1974–75
  H.C. 495   *Charity Commissioners and their Accountability*
Session 1975–76
  H.C. 621   *Policy Making in the Department of Education and*
                  Science
Session 1976–77
  H.C. 526   *The Attainments of the School Leaver*

Environment and Home Office Sub-Committee

Session 1971–72
  H.C. 47   *Probation and After Care*
Session 1972–73
  H.C. 57   *Urban Transport Planning*
  H.C. 349   *House Improvement Grants*
Session 1974
  H.C. 269   *Public Expenditure on Transport*
Session 1974–75
  H.C. 348   *Redevelopment of the London Dockland*
  H.C. 616   *New Towns*
Session 1975–76
  H.C. 433   *National Parks and the Countryside*
  H.C. 466   *Planning Procedures*
Sessions 1976–77
  H.C. 35   *Planning Procedures*

Employment and Social Services Sub-Committee

Session 1971–72
  H.C. 172   *National Health Service Facilities for Private Patients*
Session 1972–73
  H.C. 148   *Youth Employment Services*
  H.C. 182   *Employment of Women*
  H.C. 214   *Employment Services and Training*
Session 1973–74
  H.C. 115   *Accident and Emergency Services*

Session 1974
   H.C. 307   *Expenditure Cuts in Health and Personal Social Services*
   H.C. 310   *Police Recruitment and Wastage*
Session 1974–75
   H.C. 534   *The Children and Young Persons Act 1969*
Session 1975–76
   H.C. 312   *DHSS Statistics*
Session 1976–77
   H.C. 169   *Preventive Medicine*
   H.C. 394   *The Job Creation Programme*

Whole Committee
Session 1976–77
   H.C. 466   *Selected Public Expenditure Programmes*

Appendix C
List of Specialist Advisers

General Sub-Committee

1970–76	Wynne Godley, Department of Applied Economics, University of Cambridge.
1974	Professor A. A. Walters, London School of Economics and Political Science
1974	T. M. Ward, Department of Applied Economics, Cambridge
1975–76	P. M. Oppenheimer, Christ Church, University of Oxford
1976–77	T. Ward
1976–77	G. Heywood ⎫ Duncan Fraser & C. M. J. Day ⎭
	Nevil Johnson, Nuffield College, Oxford
	T. A. E. Layborne
	Professor F. F. Ridley, Liverpool University
	David Shapiro, Brunel University

Defence and External Affairs Sub-Committee

1970–76	Brigadier Kenneth Hunt, Institute of Strategic Studies
1975	Rear Admiral E. F. Gueritz

Environment and Home Office Sub-Committee

1972–75	Mr David Starkie, Reading University
1974–75	Mr Murray Stewart, University of Kent
	Mr R. G. O. Dixon, Reading University
1975–76	Mr H. W. E. Davies, Associate of Hugh Wilson and Lewis Womersley Chartered Architects and Town Planners

Trade and Industry Sub-Committee

1971–72   Mr Stuart Holland, University of Sussex
1972–73   Mr John Knight, St Edmund Hall, Oxford
1974–75   Mr Garel Rhys, University College, Cardiff
          Mr David Starkie, Reading University
          (Also before the enquiry into *The Motor Vehicle Industry*
          Professor H. A. F. Turner, Churchill College, Cambridge,
          Dr W. E. J. McCarthy, Nuffield College, Oxford and Mr
          Graham Turner)
1975–76   Mr Garel Rhys and Caroline Joll, University College,
          Cardiff.
          Peter Ainger and Anthony Thorne, Price Waterhouse

Social Services and Employment Sub-Committee

1977   Mr Rudolf Klein, Centre for Social Policy

Education and Arts Sub-Committee

1973–74   Professor Gareth Williams, Lancaster University
1975–76   Professor Gareth Williams, Lancaster University and
          Professor Maurice Kogan, Brunel University

Appendix D
List of Debates on Expenditure Committee Reports

Session 1971–72   (830) Cols 1433–1465, 9 February 1972, 2 hrs 10 min.
Report Debated: Probation and After Care
(842) Cols 1268–1368, 7 August 1972, 4 hrs 45 min.
Report debated: Defence and External Affairs

Session 1972–73   (859) Cols 1047–1119, 9 July 1973, 3 hrs 31 min.*
Report debated: Urban Transport Planning
(859) Cols 119–1166, 9 July 1973, 2 hrs 7 min.*
Report debated: Further and Higher Education

Session 1973–74   (867) Cols 372–417, 15 January 1974, 2 hrs 28 min.
Report debated: Employment Services and Training
The Employment of Women*
Youth Employment Services

Session 1974–75   (891) Cols 747–788, 1 May 1975, 2 hrs 6 min.*
Report debated: Public Expenditure on Transport
(894) Cols 827–941, 10 July 1975, 2 hrs 26 min.*
Report debated: Police Recruitment and Wastage
(894) Cols 760–827, 10 July 1975, 3 hrs 6 min.*
Report debated: Postgraduate Education
Education Maintenance Allowances

Session 1975–76   (909) Cols 1229–1337, 13 April 1976, 5 hrs 32 min.*
Report debated: Children and Young Persons Act, 1969

Debates on the Role of the Expenditure Committee

Session 1970–71   (806) Cols 618–735, 12 November 1970, 6 hrs.
On Motion to take note of the Green Paper on Select Committees, Cmnd 4507

Session 1973–74   (867) Cols 417–490, 15 January 1974, 3 hrs 44 min.
On Role of the Expenditure Committee

* (Supply Day Debates)

Bibliography

Abbreviations

APSR   American Political Science Review
BJPS   British Journal of Political Science
PS   Political Studies

Books and Articles

Anderson, James, *Public Policy Making*, Nelson, London, 1975.
Bachrach, P. and M. S. Baratz, 'Two Faces of Power', *APSR*, 61 (1966), 947–52.
Bahl, Roy, 'Studies on Determinants of Public Expenditure: A Review', in S. J. Miskin and J. F. Cotton, *Functional Federalism*, State–Local Finances Project, George Washington University, Washington, D.C., 1968.
Bator, Frances M., *The Question of Government Spending*, Harper & Row, New York, 1960.
Bell, Daniel, 'The Public Household', *The Public Interest*, 37 (1974), 29–65.
Bell, David J., *Power Influence and Authority*, Oxford University Press, New York, 1975.
Booms, Bernard H., and James R. Halldorson, 'The Politics of Redistribution: a Reformulation', *APSR*, 67 (1973, 924–33.
Braybrooke, David and Charles E. Lindblom, *A Strategy of Decision: Policy Evaluation as a Social Process*, Macmillan, London, 1963.
Breton, Albert, *The Economic Theory of Representative Government*, Macmillan, London, 1975.
Burkhead, J. and J. Miner, *Public Expenditure*, Macmillan, London, 1971.
Byrne, Paul, 'The Expenditure Committee: A Preliminary Assessment', *Parliamentary Affairs*, 27 (1974), 273–86.
Chubb, Basil, *The Control of Public Expenditure*, Oxford University Press, London, 1952.
Cnudde, Charles F. and D. McCrone, 'Party Competition and Welfare Policies in the American States', *APSR*, 63 (1969), 858–66.
Coombes, David, *The Member of Parliament and the Administration*, Allen & Unwin, London, 1966.
Coombes, David (ed), *The Power of the Purse*, P.E.P., Allen & Unwin, London, 1975.
Crossman, Richard, *Diaries of a Cabinet Minister*, vols 1 and 2, Hamish Hamilton and Jonathan Cape, London, 1975 and 1976.
Davis, Otto, N. A. H. Dempster and Aaron Wildavsky, 'A Theory of the Budgetary Process', *APSR*, 60 (1966), 529–47.
Dawson, R. E., and J. A. Robinson, 'Inter-party Competition, Economic Variables and Welfare Policies in the American States', *Journal of Politics*, 25 (1963), 265–89.

Diamond, Lord, *Public Expenditure in Practice*, Allen & Unwin, London, 1975.

Dicey, A. V., *Law and Opinion in England*, Macmillan, London, 1905.

Downs, Anthony, *An Economic Theory of Democracy*, Harper & Row, New York, 1957.

Downs, Anthony, 'Why the Government Budget is too Small in a Democracy', *World Politics*, xii (1960), 541–63.

Du Cann, Edward, *Parliament and the Purse Strings: How to Bring Public Expenditure under Parliamentary Control*, Conservative Political Centre, London, 1977.

Dye, Thomas, *Politics, Economics and the Public*, Rand McNally, Chicago, 1966.

Einzig, Paul, *The Control of the Purse*, Secker & Warburg, London, 1959.

Ellwood, John L. and James A. Thurber, 'The New Congressional Budget Process: the Hows and Whys of House–Senate Differences', in Lawrence C. Doad and Bruce I. Oppenheim (eds), *Congress Reconsidered*, Praeger, New York, 1977.

Fenno, Richard, *The Power of the Purse: Appropriations Politics in Congress*, Little Brown, Boston, 1966.

Fenno, Richard, *Congressmen in Committees*, Little Brown, Boston, 1973.

Fry, Brian R., and Richard F. Winters, 'The Politics of Redistribution', *APSR*, 64 (1970), 508–22.

Galbraith, K., *The Affluent Society*, Houghton Mifflin, Boston, 1958.

Greenwood, R., C. R. Hinings and S. Ranson, 'Budgetary Processes in English Local Government', *Political Studies*, xxv (1977), 25–47.

Griffiths, Ernest S., *Congress: Its Contemporary Role*, 4th edition, New York University Press, New York, 1967.

Heclo, Hugh, 'Review Article: Policy Analysis', *BJPS*, 2 (1972), 83–108.

Heclo, Hugh and Aaron Wildavsky, *The Private Government of Public Spending*, Macmillan, London, 1974.

Hofferbert, Richard I., 'The Relation Between Public Policy and Some Structural and Environmental Variables in the American States', *APSR*, 60 (1966), 73–82.

Hyder, M., 'Parliament and Defence Affairs', *Public Administration*, 55 (1977), 59–78.

Hill, Andrew and Anthony Whichelow, *What's Wrong with Parliament?*, Penguin, London, 1964.

Johnson, Nevil, *Parliament and Administration: The Estimates Committee 1945–65*. Allen & Unwin, London, 1966.

Klein, Rudolf, *et al.*, *Social Policy and Public Expenditure 1974*, Centre for Studies in Social Policy, London, 1974.

Klein, Rudolf, (ed), *Inflation and Priorities 1975*, Centre for Studies in Social Policy, London, 1975.

Klein, Rudolf, 'The Politics of Public Expenditure: American Theory and British Practice', *BJPS*, 6 (1976), 401–32.

Lee, Michael, 'Select Committees and the Constitution', *Political Quarterly*, 41 (1970).

Lindblom, Charles E., 'The Science of Muddling Through', *Public Administration Review*, 19 (1959), 79–88.

Lindblom, Charles E., 'Decision Making in Taxation and Expenditure', in *Public Finances: Needs, Sources and Utilisation*, National Bureau of Economic Research, Princeton, 1961.

Lindblom, Charles E., *The Intelligence of Democracy*, Macmillan, London, 1965.

Lord, Guy, *The French Budgetary Process*, Berkeley, California, 1973.

Lowi, T., *The End of Liberalism*, Norton, New York, 1969.

Lukes, Stephen, *Power: A Radical View*, Macmillan, London, 1974.

Mackintosh, John P., *The British Cabinet*, Stevens, London, 1962.

Manley, John F., *The Politics of Finance: The House Committee on Ways and Means*, Little Brown, Boston, 1970.

McKeen, Roland, *Public Spending*, McGraw Hill, New York, 1968.

Members of the Study of Parliament Group, *Specialist Committees in the British Parliament: The Experience of a Decade*, P.E.P., June 1976, vol. xlii, no. 564.

Mill, J. S., *On Representative Government*, Everyman Edition, London, 1948, First published 1861.

Morris, Alfred (ed), *The Growth of Parliamentary Scrutiny by Committee*, Pergamon, Oxford, 1970.

Musgrave, Richard, *Fiscal Systems*, McGraw Hill, New York, 1969.

Musgrave, Richard, 'A Multiple Theory of Budget Determination', *Finanzarchiv*, 1957, Vol. 333–43.

Newton, K., 'The Politics of Public Expenditure Studies', *Political Studies*, 25 (1977), 122–27.

Niskanen, William, *Bureaucracy and Representative Government*, Aldine-Atherton, New York, 1971.

Niskanen, William, *Bureaucracy: Servant or Master?*, The Institute for Economic Affairs, London, 1973.

O'Connor, James, *The Fiscal Crisis of the State*, St Martin's Press, New York, 1973.

Olson, Mancur, *The Logic of Collective Action: Public Goods and the Theory of Groups*, Harvard University Press, Cambridge Mass., 1965.

Owen, David, 'Parliamentary Control of Defence Budgeting', *Brassey's Annual*, London, 1973.

Parsons, Talcott, 'On the Concept of Influence', *Public Opinion Quarterly*, 27 (1963).

Peacock, Alan and Jack Wiseman, *The Growth of Public Expenditure*, Allen & Unwin, London, 1961.

Proxmire, William, *Can Congress Control Spending?* American Enterprise Institute, Washington D.C., 1973.

Pryor, Frederick, *Public Expenditure in Communist and Capitalist Nations*, Richard Irwin, Homewood, Illinois, 1968.

Ranney, Austin (ed), *Political Science and Public Policy*, Chicago, 1968.

Reid, Gordon, *The Politics of Financial Control*, Hutchinson, London, 1966.

Rogers, William, Crosland Memorial Lecture, 1977.

Roseveare, Henry, *The Treasury*, Allen Lane, London, 1969.

Ryle, Michael, 'Parliamentary Control of Expenditure and Taxation', *Political Quarterly*, 37 (1967), 435–46.

Sandford, Cedric and Paul Dean, 'Public Expenditure: Why It Has Grown', *The Banker*, April 1970, 370–87.

Sandford, Cedric and Ann Robinson, 'Public Spending', *The Banker*, November 1975, 1241–54.

Schick, Allen, 'The Congressional Budget and Impoundment Control Act, PL 93–344: a summary of Its Provisions', Congressional Research Service, Library of Congress, Washington D.C., 5 February 1975.

Schultze, Charles E., *The Politics and Economics of Public Spending*, The Brookings Institution, Washington D.C., 1968.

Sharkansky, Ira, *The Politics of Taxing and Spending*, Bobbs-Merrill, Indianapolis and New York, 1969.

Sharkansky, Ira and Richard I. Hofferbert, 'Dimensions of State Politics, Economics and Public Policy', *APSR*, 63 (1969), 867–79.

Silkin, Arthur, 'The Expenditure Committee: a New Development?', *Public Administration*, 53 (1975), 45–66.

Tomkins, Gary L., 'A Causal Model of State Welfare Expenditures', *Journal of Politics*, 37 (1975), 392–416.

Walkland, S. A., 'The Politics of Parliamentary Reform', *Parliamentary Affairs*, xxix (1976), 190–210.

Walkland, S. A. and Michael Ryle (eds), *The Commons in the Seventies*, Fontana, London, 1977.

Wheare, K. C., *Government by Committee*, Clarendon Press, Oxford, 1955.

Wildavsky, Aaron, *The Politics of the Budgetary Process*, Little Brown, Boston, 1964.

Wildavsky, Aaron, *Budgeting: A Comparative Theory of the Budgetary Process*, Little Brown, Boston, 1975.

Wright, Maurice, 'Public Expenditure in Britain: The Crisis of Control', *Public Administration*, 55 (1977), 143–70.

House of Commons Papers and Government Publications

1. Sixth Report from the Select Committee on Estimates, *Treasury Control of Expenditure*, H.C. 254–1, of 1957–58.

2. *Report of the Committee on the Control of Public Expenditure*, (the Plowden Report), Cmnd 1432, July 1961.

3. Report of the Select Committee on Procedure, *Specialist Committees*, H.C. 303 of 1964–65.

4. Report of the Select Committee on Procedure, *Financial Procedure*, H.C. 122 of 1965–66.

5. Report of the Select Committee on Procedure, *The Control of Public Expenditure and Administration*, H.C. 410 of 1968–69.

6. *Public Expenditure: A New Presentation*, Cmnd 4017, April 1969.

7. *Select Committees of the House of Commons*, Cmnd 4507, October 1970.

Index

180   *Parliament and Public Spending*